THE GREAT RETREAT

The Nez Perces War
in Words and Pictures

by Pascal Tchakmakian

CHRONICLE BOOKS/SAN FRANCISCO

Printed in the United States of America

Library of Congress Cataloging in Publication Data

Tchakmakian, Pascal
  The great retreat.

  1. Nez Percé Indians—Wars, 1877.   I. Title.
E83.877.T33   973.8'2   76-21280
ISBN 0-87701-077-3

Chronicle Books
870 Market Street
San Francisco, Ca. 94102

Contents

N
↑

Nez Perce Route ▬▬▬▬▬▬
Miles's Route ••••••••••••••••••••
Battles ⊗

C A N

Bitterroot

■ Fort Missoula

Snake   River

North
Clearwater   Fork
River   Orofino Cr.

Kamiah Crossing   Lolo Pass

■
Fort Lapwai   Middle
Fork   Mountains

Selway

⊗
Battle of   Battle of
the Clearwater   the Big Hole

South Fork   ⊗

Ronde   River

Wallowa   Salmon   River   Big Hole   Jeffer

Grande   River   River

Virginia C

▲▲ O R E G O N
▲▲ Blue
▲▲ Mountains

Snake

River

Lemhi ●

T E R R I T O R Y   T E R R I T O R Y   I D A H O

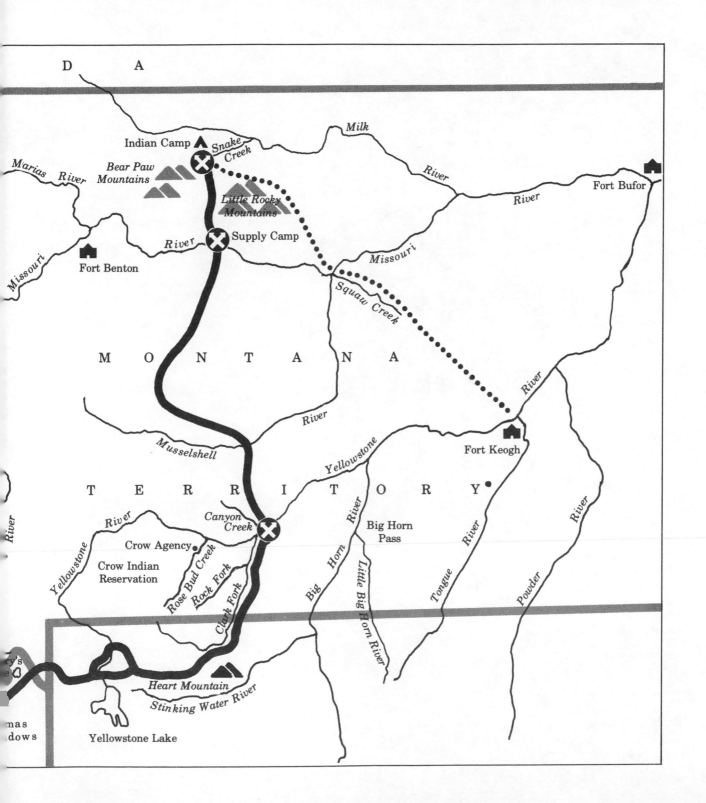

Preface

The preface to William Brandon's *Book of Indians* includes a quote by the late John F. Kennedy, which expresses the spirit with which the author wrote this study of the white man's war on the Nez Perces:

> Before we can set out on the road
> to success, we have to know where
> we are going, and before we can
> know that, we must determine where
> we have been in the past. It seems
> a basic requirement to study the
> history of our Indian people.
> America has much to learn about the
> heritage of our American Indians.
> Only through this study can we, as a
> nation, do what must be done if our
> treatment of the American Indian is
> not to be marked down for all time
> as a national disgrace.

The author is especially grateful to Mr. Brandon and to L. V. McWhorter, whose three works were invaluable in the research and preparation of this manuscript. A special note of thanks is offered to Earle Connette of the Washington State University Library for many of the fine photographs from their extensive McWhorter collection and to Jim Davis of the Idaho State Historical Museum for his help in selecting photographs from their Nez Perce files. Among the many other references used by the author of events in the Nez Perces history were occasionally given several different interpretations. The author was forced to select, whether rightly or wrongly, the source which seemed to him closest to the truth.

A number of persons contributed valuable advice and assistance during the research and manuscript stages of the book. Acknowledgement is directed to the Caxton Printers, Ltd. of Caldwell, Idaho, for their interest; M.F. for rare books; Sally Waldox for proofreading; the staff of the Peabody Museum of Harvard and the Museum of American Indians in New York for providing references, Alma Nahiagian for editing, and Ethelyn Churchill for revision, re-typing and encouragement.

*The Nez Perces had a personal and religious responsibility
to leave the world as unspoiled as they had found it.*

1.

The Coming of the Crowned Ones

In the beginning, there was land. There was the sun. And there were all sorts of people. Once, some thousands of snows ago, a huge monster came about this land and began eating all those good people. They implored Itsy-yi-yi, or Coyote, to help them. The good Coyote came and, disguised as one of the good people, was swallowed by the huge monster. Once inside the monster's body, Coyote began tearing the inside of the monster. The monster, feeling pain, begged the great Coyote to exit, but Coyote continued his deadly work until the monster died. Leaving the body triumphantly, Coyote continued tearing it apart, and from each part, he made one of the tribes. From the feet came the Blackfeet to the northeast. From the head came the Sioux and the Cheyenne. All the body was divided and all the tribes were created. But the heart was left on the ground. Taking that vital part, Coyote created the Nez Perces, known as Nimapu, or "The Real People."

TWO or three generations before the arrival of the Lewis and Clark expedition in October 1805, a Nez Perce prophet by the name of Schowsap had prophesied that men with white skin would sweep over their land and conquer it. As human nature goes, the prophecy lost much of its original impact and was remembered only as the promise of white-skinned visitors who would possess powerful medicine. Thus, when word came that the first white men were arriving, the Nez Perces were more excited than frightened or hostile. Talk among the tribes had already reassured them that the white men far to the east were generally peaceful, that they were eager traders, and that they carried and sold weapons—firearms—which would make the Indian possessor the master of his territory and his enemies. The Nez Perce name "Shoyapoo," or "Crowned Ones," was given to these new people both because of their reputed superiority and because they wore strange tall caps of racoon fur.

The Lewis and Clark expedition stopped with the Nez Perces both enroute to and returning from their destination, the shores of the Great Water in the west. On the return trip, the snows had begun, so the white explorers remained as guests of the Nez Perces for the duration of the winter. Friendship and mutual respect quickly developed between the two peoples. The whites were impressed by the order, industry, civility and high intelligence of the Nez Perces nation. The Indians admired the discipline, the genius for healing, and the astounding technology (the magnets and spy-glasses and rifles) which the Shoyapoos brought with them. The Nez Perces were not a tradition-bound people, and they saw in the white way of life some possibilities for the improvement of the lot of their own people.

Perhaps most impressive of all was the white strangers' reverence and enthusiasm for their God and for their "Book of Heaven" in which all knowledge and all success and happiness might be found. The Nez Perces were noted among the tribes as an intensely religious people. Now, the whites spoke of the "right manner" for the worship of God and for the attainment of eternal life in paradise after death. They persuaded many of the Nez Perces elders of the error in their worship of nature, and they boasted of the earthly rewards that might come to the Indians if they were to embrace Christianity. At the eager insistence of all of the Nez Perces spokesmen, the white men promised that they would soon send Christian teachers and many copies of the magical "Book of Heaven." The white expedition embarked, then, toward the Missouri, and life among the Nez Perces returned to normal. However, there were many in the tribe, particularly among the leaders, who remembered the white men's promise and who waited impatiently for their return.

For unknown thousands of years, an unwritten law, tacitly respected by all Indians of the Northwest, ruled that Nez Perces

A Nez Perce woman

lands began at the foot of the Yellowstone—"the land of the shooting waters." Northward, they extended to the land of the Coeur d'Alenes and the Bitterroots range; south, to the Snake River and the Salmon; and westward, to the Blue Mountains. Shut in by several mountain ranges, winters in the Nez Perces sanctuary were mild, summers hot, the springs and falls lush and comfortable. In the many valleys, where the Nez Perces bands pitched their villages, the rich, sun-drenched meadows and icy cold mountain waters provided a natural haven for game, for the buffalo, and for raising herds of horses which could be traded to nearby tribes.

According to the ancient religious beliefs of the Nez Perces, everything within their purview was God-made and sacred to mankind: the fragrant blue camas flowers, whose soft bulb root was steamed and then mashed and dried as a winter staple; the muscular salmon which were netted in the Salmon and Snake rivers and dried in the summer sun; the forests of huckleberries and gooseberries, which were harvested in the heat of August; the immense herds of buffalo and elk and the handsome, agile Appaloosa horses which the Indians had bred and nurtured; the sunflower seeds and skunk cabbage; the beaver and the elusive bighorn sheep; the Douglas fir, which had been worshipped in centuries past, and the sandbar willow, which was woven by the women into baskets, dishes, and the hats and decorated pouches favored by many other tribes.

For everything of importance in the Nez Perces world, there was a spirit and a ceremony of thanks to that spirit and to the Creator. And each Nez Perce had a personal, religious responsibility to leave the world, after his death, as intact and unspoiled as he had found it at birth. Even warfare followed a code of conservation and gentility. Killing an enemy in battle was almost tantamount to murder, and a Nez Perce could be sentenced to life-long exile from the tribe for such an offense. The Nez Perces' respect for individuality and human life, their worship of nature and ancestral spirits, were as reverent, as integrated, as valuable a religion as any society could claim.

Decades passed after the Lewis and Clark expedition had left the

Nez Perces lands in May 1806, and during that span, a mere scattering of white men—French trappers, English traders, Yankee mountain men—passed through Nez Perces territory. Year after year, the Nez Perces waited impatiently for the teachers of the Book of Heaven. For more than a quarter of a century, they had told and retold the story of the white expedition, the vows of peace, and the promise of Christian power and knowledge which, they believed, would make them the equal of the white men. Finally, in the year 1836, the first white preachers came. Most of the Nez Perces bands were camped together on a large, gently sloping meadow which was blue with camas blossoms. Old Joseph, the head chief of the Wallowa band, was first to hear the news from riders. "The white teachers are coming."

A council was called immediately. Nez Perce life demanded a council for nearly every important event. The custom gave each of the elders and leaders a voice and a vote in the decisions of the tribe. At the same time, one leader was chosen as the spokesman or decision-maker—the Chief—for a particular event, whether a buffalo hunt, a battle, or a trade council. Contrary to white impressions, there was never one iron chief whose word was law in all matters.

Each speaker gave his point of view to the assembly of patriarchal elders and proven warriors sitting around a fire in the beautiful dusk of an autumn night. The oratory lasted well into the night, and the highlight was the eloquent debate between Too-Hool-Hool-Zute, a brave noted for his mind and excellent speech, and Yellow Bull, an older chief trained by Old Joseph in the art of exposing facts and, from these facts, drawing a logical conclusion.

Too-Hool, that night, surpassed himself in his poetic celebration of the ancient lore and traditions—and religion—of Nez Perces. He referred again and again to the organic cycles of life, to the sky and their brothers and the mountains and rivers, to father sun and mother earth. He gently ridiculed the rest of the assembly for their eagerness to embrace the white ways and their strange beliefs. He asked them how they could so blithely turn away from the faith that had sustained their fathers and their fathers' fathers.

But Old Joseph and Yellow Bull uncovered fact after fact: The white man is already in the land of the Cheyenne. He is coming here. Rumors have already spread from the Sioux, the Cheyennes, the Blackfeet and other eastern tribes that white men were wiping out whole herds of buffalo with their firearms. They were also spreading like a prairie fire over Indian lands and building houses and fences upon these lands. The Nez Perces had heard word of Christian teachers—preachers—who had stopped briefly with the Flatheads, but then found the Flathead country too hard, too poor, and moved on very shortly to the territory of the Willamette. There they had preached and established a mission, but they were also accommodating themselves with choice lands and bringing in other white settlers as well.

The wisdom of Brother Too-Hool is beyond question, Yellow Bull agreed. But the white man is already in the land of the Cheyenne. We must welcome them and prepare to adopt some of their ways if we are to survive this invasion. Yellow Bull reminded his listeners that it is far easier to embrace your enemies than to conquer them. The word "enemy" was not used, but the idea of a "coming force" was understood.

Old Chief Joseph also spoke of the whites as a reality with which the Nez Perces must reckon. But he was not resigned to gloomy forecasts. The rumors had also brought back tales of prosperous mission villages in which the Indians were supplied with seeds and cloth, with iron tools and utensils, with firearms for hunting, and with warm, dry structures during the winter snows. Too-Hool vehemently objected to the benefits of farming—How could anyone plough the earth which we have called Mother for untold generations?—but Old Joseph could answer that cultivated fields had eliminated the lean periods of winter and had allowed the mission Indians to remain securely in one campsite through the bad weather. And this stability allowed schooling. Above all, Old Joseph was enthusiastic about the miracles of the new religion and the wondrous skills of reading and writing which the mission Indians were taught.

The council finally ended with the decision to welcome the white

*Chief Yellow Bull believed in accepting,
rather than fighting the white settlers.*

missionaries without qualification. The promise had been made by Lewis and Clark nearly 30 years ago. The Nez Perces' experience with whites had been peaceful and mutually beneficial. The traditional lore of the tribe spoke of the powerful medicine which would come to the Nez Perces with the white visitors. And then there was the Book of Heaven and the blessings that it would bring. Perhaps most endearing to the Indians was the fact that the missionaries had traveled for many months, from far beyond the Sioux territory, to live with and teach the Nez Perces.

Old Joseph, and representatives from all the bands, made the three-day journey up the valley to meet the missionaries and guide them through the mountains, where, high up, it was just beginning to snow. The two missionary couples, the Spaldings and the Whitmans, were led into the rich green valleys of the Nez Perces and settled in the Lapwai region. They were given teepees, robes, food, and constant care and attendance by a steady stream of Indians traveling to Lapwai to help them and to learn from them. A young Nez Perces who had once been to a white man's school in the east acted as interpreter until the missionaries and the Indians were able to communicate in a halting combination of Shahaptian and English.

Whitman, an ascetic and somewhat distant man, was very different in manner from the rugged, bearded Spalding, whose eyes ever-burned with the fire of impatient energy and religious fervor. The Indians were surprised that the two men represented the same religion. They were not so surprised when, after several days, the couples split, Spalding remaining at Lapwai while Whitman and his wife left to settle further west in the Walla-Walla Valley.

The white men had spent much of their time in those several days riding about the Nez Perce territory, surveying the land and arguing loudly in their own language. Whitman, it became apparent, was primarily interested in the acquisition of land and the saving of heathen souls, whereas Spalding, though also acquisitive, was hard-working and sincerely interested in benefiting the Indians by introducing farming and traditional Yankee values into their nomadic way of life. Spalding's religious zealotry may

Nez Perces prior to the war of 1877.

well have been tempered by his gentle wife, who immediately began schooling the Nez Perces youngsters and was primarily responsible for the publication of a Bible in the Shahaptian language.

The presence of the missionaries had immediate effects on the life patterns of the Nez Perces. For the first time in centuries of Nez Perces history, there were uncertainties. In the past, the tribe knew exactly where everyone would be and what they should and would be doing according to the time of year, their needs, their age, their status. The chieftains within each band had always had inviolate authority within their territories and according to their roles as judges or medicine men, warriors or hunters.

Now, the bands were crossing one another's territories in disordered patterns, some going north to Lapwai or to the Whitman settlement at Walla-Walla, others following the habits of centuries and journeying as usual to the root-digging grounds or to the buffalo hunt. After the first winter with the missionaries, when the deep snows had melted on the mountaintops and the streams were roaring, Old Joseph himself had set the example and led his band from their beloved Wallowa Valley to Lapwai and a new way of life. He wanted to be among the first to learn how to read and write and to embrace the Christian faith. He also wished to preserve his tribe and was shrewdly conscious of what the future could bring should they refuse to change. He understood the danger that gradually but surely approached from the east.

At first, some of the Indian leaders, particularly the medicine men, waged a quiet verbal war with the newcomers. They resented the rigid new standards of behavior promulgated by the white men—the "laws," as they called them, which recognized private possession of land, harsh punishments for wrongdoing, and other concepts confusing to a people who lived by the natural laws of mutual respect and responsibility for one another and for the sacred land which was their mother. They were wary of the strong influence of the Christians over many of their people, who were discarding their ancient ways with merely the promise of better ones to come. They deplored the foolishness of families who became

*Marcus and Narcissa Whitman—early missionaries
who were more interested in acquiring land than saving souls.*

convinced that Christian salvation was synonymous with the miracle of an earthly paradise. For the first time in hundreds of generations, there were beggars among the Nez Perces—individuals and even whole families who gathered near the missions, waiting for miracles and depending upon the white men for food and clothing and shelter. In the past, the tribe had fed the tribe, and no one could suffer privation while others prospered.

Spalding's booming voice demanded change after change in the old ways of the tribe. No one was to work on Sunday. The traditions of hunting and gathering were condemned, and the sanctity of the soil, of mother earth, was violated by the plough and the hoe. No man could possess more than one woman, and the union of a man and woman was a sin until it had been ordained with a Christian marriage.

Raising the Book of Heaven over his head, Spalding returned again and again to the concepts of sin and an eternal punishment called "Hell." The introduction of farming had already sharply divided the tribe—many of the warrior chiefs considered yeomanry an affront to nature and the job of "half men." The matter of Hell and a punishing God further confused the Nez Perces. Some accepted the white men's faith and fear of God to the letter. Others retained the reasoning, which had sustained them for centuries, that a sin is only a moment of weakness or ignorance when a man "is not quite himself." For each error, there was usually a definite way to correct it. If a man stole, he would give back what he had taken and thereby re-establish his honesty. The Nez Perces had never believed that a man could learn from too cruel a punishment.

Nor could they understand how an "Omnipresent, Omniscient, Everloving Creator of all Things" could invent such a thing as Hell for those who had erred (or who had not followed the right religion, as the Christians claimed). The doubters among the Nez Perces soon formulated a more comfortable myth which fit their own ideas of God's justice: When a good man dies, his spirit goes straight to the Akunkenekoo, the white man's Heaven; When a sinful or ignorant man dies, God asks that spirit to follow a long and tiring road, though he, too, finally reaches Heaven. God loves all men. The high-pitched voice of Too-Hool was raised again and again, like a sacred chant, to protest the religion brought by the missionaries. To argue of Heaven and Hell, he said, or to marry our women or uproot the sacred meadows will not add a single buffalo to the plain, nor one golden shaft of light to the sun.

The resistance of some of the tribe to the white religion and the white way of life was for a long time muted by the evident successes of the people who, like Old Joseph, followed the teachings of the missionaries. The green sprouts of corn and potatoes waving in the springtime breezes began to free the Indians from the hard life of hunting and grubbing. Spalding established a mill and bought a small number of sheep from the Hudson Bay Company. The potent medicine of Mr. Whitman and Mrs. Spalding saved many of the Nez Perces children from disfiguring diseases and death.

Some of the warriors scoffed at Old Joseph, who studied the holy words of the Christians in Mrs. Spalding's classroom among the small children, including his own daughter and son. But scoffers also found themselves looking on in awed silence as the old man sat for hours by the light of the evening fire, painstakingly copying the alphabet he had been taught. These signs, he explained, can be understood by anyone forever. They do not change to suit me or you or him. They do not fade in meaning with the passing of the seasons and the fogs that muddle an old man's head.

When the first wagon train of 20 white people crossed the Nez Perces lands, enroute to the Willamette, this too seemed at first a boon to the tribe. They rode to the train and, following the example of the Spaldings, exchanged goods and livestock with the travelers. In a very few years, the enterprising Nez Perces, with their talent for horse-breeding and trading, became one of the richest of the Western tribes. Soon, however, those 20 people became hundreds, and they no longer simply crossed the Nez Perces lands but began to settle in the fertile river valleys adjacent to the ancient territory of the tribe.

The Reverend Whitman aided this emigration and enriched himself by writing articles for Eastern periodicals and then traveling to the East to lecture on the glories of the Oregon Territory.

He, Spalding, and numerous new entrepreneurs in the area then sold or rented land—Indian land—to the settlers. If there was ever any direct payment to the Indians for the land, the transactions were seldom if ever just. Most often, the purchases were merely promises never to be fulfilled. The Indians had been drilled for years in the Christian tenets of brotherhood and equality and justice. Yet now they were told that in the white courts of law, they could not prove that they *owned* these lands of their ancestors.

By the mid-1840s, the Nez Perces had become accustomed to the sight of virtually endless streams of wagons meandering along the landscape. One year, an immense train with nearly a thousand people arrived from the southeast, slowly treking along the now well-rutted trail. With the new settlers came alcohol, small pox, firearms, and daily turmoil. Game—the deer, beaver, big horns and buffalo—were decimated. Streams were diverted or polluted. The ancient fields of kouse and camas, staples to the Indians, were trampled and uprooted. Worst of all, and utterly inexplicable to the tribe, the settlers fenced the land and objected vigorously, even violently, to trespassers. With appalling irony, little more than a decade after they had made the grueling journey to bring education and Christianity to the Indians, the white men had decided that the Indian was a nuisance. White faces became the majority in dozens of new congregations formed by missionaries more intent on acreage than on the souls of the heathen Indians.

The Nez Perces territory was still vast enough to allow the encroachers and the tribe to live without conflict, but tensions and incidents became more frequent. Problems among the Nez Perces themselves also became more common. Many individuals and several bands had become disgusted with the changes, rejecting the white man's hypocritical religion and retiring to the hills or remote valleys, where they restored the old ways and adopted the odd, messianic new Dreamers' faith, an anti-white, anti-Christian nature worship which had become popular among many of the Western Indian tribes. These non-Christian Nez Perces, as they came to be categorized, were outcasts in the eyes of their brothers who remained faithful Christians, cutting their hair to the white

Christian Nez Perces cut their hair to the white man's length
and adopted white man's clothes as symbols of their religious conversion.

man's length as a symbol of their religious fealty. Traditionally, a Nez Perce cut his braided hair only upon the death of a loved one. Thus, the sight of the shorn tribesmen told better than a thousand philosophical council arguments how bands, even individual families among the Nez Perces had become estranged by their religious differences and their capitulation to white dominance.

Old Joseph, who headed the largest and wealthiest of the bands, remained faithful to the white religion and to the more advantageous aspects of the white man's ways. He had been baptized and married to his wife in a Christian ceremony in 1839. He had dropped his tribal name of Tuekakes, "The Oldest Grizzly," in favor of Joseph—Old Joseph when his young son and heir was renamed after him.

Had Joseph dismantled his teepee at Lapwai and moved south, back into the Wallowa, only a handful of Nez Perces, from all of the bands, would have remained at the mission. The other Christian chiefs, Lawyer, James, Jason, and Timothy, did not have the respect which he had garnered over the years with his intelligent, far-sighted and careful leadership. Old Joseph maintained his belief in the new way of life, partly because of the skills taught by Mrs. Spalding and the advantages of farming, and herding (he had seen with his own eyes the rapidly dwindling herds of buffalo). But, more important, the aging chief perceived the dangerous position of his tribe, surrounded by a force of white settlers who increased in numbers and strength every day. Already, small contingents of white soldiers had visited the area and established posts within a few days' ride. In council, he repeated his belief often: To avoid conquest, and perhaps even annihilation, one must learn to imitate the potential enemy.

The original Lapwai Indian Agency.

2.

A Divided, Angry World

AN epidemic of measles broke out in 1847 among the Cayuses, a tribe to the north of Lapwai. Rumors had reached the Nez Perces the previous years that the Cayuses were dying in large numbers from a strange white man's disease. Soon, witnesses confirmed in council that the tribe, already humiliated by the loss of most of their lands to the whites, were now reduced to a small, desperate band by the combination of a ferocious winter and the spread of the fever. Neither the tribal medicine men, nor Whitman, the nearest missionary, had effected any change in the deadliness of the disease among the weakened tribe, and the Cayuses were convinced, understandably, that the epidemic had been visited on the tribe by the whites as a scheme to acquire the remaining Indian lands.

Councils were held; the medicine men cried out that the disease would end only when its source, the whites, were killed. On November 29, 1847, the Cayuses chief Tamahas and a few of his braves rode into the nearest mission, Whitman's station, and killed the minister, his wife, and a dozen more white settlers. The Cayuses then rampaged through the countryside, driving the white settlers to the east or into compounds. Spalding narrowly escaped death when he was informed of the attack while on his way to visit the Whitman mission. He turned back toward Lapwai in a desperate flight with the Cayuses band in close pursuit. The Lapwai mission had also gotten word of the attack, and Mrs. Spalding, her children, and other whites in the area were persuaded to leave the mission under the escort of the Christian Nez Perces. When the Lapwai mission was abandoned, a group of renegade Nez Perces pillaged the church and the Spalding home.

The massacre and the vandalism of the few Nez Perces stunned the whites and Nez Perces alike. No one had anticipated violence;

Whitman himself had been warned that trouble might be brewing among the Cayuses, but he had been supremely confident of his authority over the generally peaceable Indians of the area. There had been tensions between the Nez Perces and the nearest white settlers—rapes, theft, trade disagreements usually perpetrated by whites—but the strong sense of justice among the tribe and the respect which it had earned among most whites provided an atmosphere which permitted amicable settlement for such problems. Then, too, the Nez Perces had not yet borne the large-scale invasion which had nearly wiped out both the land and the people of the Cayuses tribe.

The initial effect of the Whitman massacre was hysteria among the white settlers of the Northwest. Many of them had come west from the Ohio region and the Midwest, where vicious Indian wars of a generation ago were still a vivid and frightening memory. Although all evidence was to the contrary, the whites were ready to assume that these northwestern Indians were also a bloody lot. They cried out for vengeance and protection, and for the first time, the U.S. Army moved permanent forces into the area. Missions were closed, including the Spalding enterprise at Lapwai, and the newly Christian Indians were abandoned by their mentors and sometime protectors.

For several years afterward, the area remained at peace. The Christian Nez Perces continued to follow the principles and practices of their new way of life. The white encroachers were temporarily frightened off, and the tribe prospered with trade and farming. One Indian, Red Wolf, was reported to have developed a productive orchard. The Indian agent for Oregon was glowing in his praise of their progress and made a verbal promise to the tribe that white men would not be permitted within their boundaries without permission of the Nez Perces leadership.

By the mid-1850s, two events came to alter the harmony of the Nez Perces country. One was the discovery of gold in mountain streams bordering the Nez Perces lands. Gold fever had gripped the citizenry of the United States ever since Sutter had staked a claim in the foothills of the Sierra in 1848. The possibility of another bonanza like that of California brought scores of new settlers and prospectors into the Oregon Territory. And as the lands surrounding the Nez Perces were claimed and mined for the precious metal, the gold-seekers began to cast greedy eyes upon the untouched hillsides within the Nez Perces boundaries.

The other event of note was the well-meaning decision of the territory's Governor Stevens to ratify in an official government treaty, the claims of the Nez Perces and other tribes to their ancestral lands. Stevens was not a great humanitarian by any means. He intended to extract portions of these Indian lands for white settlement and prospecting, and he probably stood to gain in some way from the transactions. Still, his official concern—a just one— was that there would eventually be serious trouble in the territory if he did not make some effort to restrict white settlement, and especially white gold-hunting, to those lands which the Indians would not consider crucial to both their livelihood and their dignity.

He reasoned that a treaty between the government and all of the Indian tribes would legally define the Indian reservations, make trespassers punishable by the federal government, and preserve the harmony of the country and the progressive attitudes and behavior of the Indians. He was also concerned with the ancient enmities and regular warfare between certain of the tribes and, again, thought that a treaty would help to define territories and bring peace and progress to the Indians.

The Nez Perces Reservation, as set out in the proposed treaty, included virtually all of the land claimed by the tribe. On the small tracts which they would surrender, they were guaranteed use of fishing stations along the Snake River and pasturing rights on any lands which remained public. No whites, with the exception of employees of the Indian Bureau, were to be permitted on the Nez Perces land without permission of the tribe; and the government agreed to furnish, in addition to cash payments, a number of new facilities—schools, mills, a blacksmith shop, a hospital—on the reservation.

The treaty was not a bad arrangement under the circumstances,

*Governor Stevens ratified the treaty which would restrict
white settlement and preserve Indian lands.*

and after much discussion and some rather unsubtle bribery of the more venal Christian chiefs the Nez Perces readily agreed to its provisions in 1855. Surrounding tribes were not so well-treated, and although they followed the Nez Perces lead and signed the agreement, they were deeply resentful both of the treaty and of the compliance of the Nez Perces. In a very short time, the hostility became a kind of guerilla warfare, and Stevens was forced to bring in more troops, as well as enlist warriors from the Christian faction of the Nez Perces.

The strange turn of events—Nez Perces in the employ of the whites and fighting their neighboring tribes—caused an even more acute estrangement between the Christian and Non-Christian (now called, as well, the Treaty and the Non-treaty) Nez Perces bands. Many of the younger men, in particular, were angry at the easy acquiescence of their elders to the demands of the whites, and some of these warriors joined the hostile tribes in raids on the white military supply trains. Even some of the elders began to doubt the wisdom of their action when the treaty became tied up in Congress, and the tribe did not receive the first payments for the land they had relinquished until nearly five years after they had signed the treaty.

The Army finally subdued the hostile tribes, and another rather more tenuous period of peace settled over the land. A Nez Perce ended that peace. Jane, the 18-year-old daughter of the Christian Chief Timothy, befriended a group of prospectors camped across the reservation border from Timothy's village. Her motivation is unknown—some say she acted at the behest of her father, who was sympathetic to the whites. Whatever her reasons, she led the group of gold-hunters along secret Indian trails across the reservation and to a creekbed, where gold was found. The strike was not significant, and the prospectors were soon discovered by Indian patrols and led peaceably out of the reservation. The men returned, however, with supplies for a winter-long stake.

Apparently because they were few in number and well-behaved, the Indians did not remove the prospectors again. The Nez Perces were concerned about settlers on their pastures and farmlands, not men who dug and panned in the streams along the scrubby hills of the back country. The following spring, the appearance of one of the miners in Walla Walla with $800 in gold dust quickly changed the situation. New miners came to the Nez Perces lands in droves.

The Bureau agent on the reservation had anticipated the problem and tried to reduce the rising tensions by convincing the Nez Perces to allow mining on these lands, which the Indians cared little about. In return, the Indians were promised that no farmers would be allowed on their lands, that the miners would not disturb their farms and meadows, and that the government would supply a small force of Army regulars to maintain order and to protect the Indian rights. The Army post was to consist of no more than two buildings—a boat landing and a warehouse.

Within a few months, the miners had spread in every direction, disregarding the boundaries which had been set for them. The small post became a village and then a town—Lewiston—named, ironically, to commemorate the expedition of Lewis and Clark, which had been sheltered by the Nez Perces. Farmland was claimed and fenced, horses were stolen, and individual Indians, especially women and the elderly, were harassed and cheated. When the angry Nez Perces protested, the whites were indignant and made counter-demands that the "devious" Indians be driven from the area. Many of these same whites had been saved from starvation the previous winter, when the Nez Perces had come to the aid of hundreds of snowbound miners.

Another treaty council was called for the spring of 1863 "to adjust the boundaries of the reservation." The Nez Perces were less compliant this time. The young men were sulking in ominous silence. The elders were sharply divided, some like Chief Lawyer, favoring the new treaty, since most of the payments and benefits were to go to his tribe. In addition, the government had promised him a salary as head chief (their title) of all of the Nez Perces bands. Others—Joseph, his son Young Joseph, and Eagle Robe and Too-Hool—refused to give up any more land. They insisted that the whites be removed and that the provisions of the previous treaty be honored. A third angry group objected to any agreement, including the treaty of 1855, and urged immediate warfare on the whites.

The argument and the council continued for days, with no compromises among the factions. Finally, the chiefs agreed to make individual decisions and to negotiate separate treaties for each band. In this way, they hoped that each could gain advantages for his village and none would be bound by the agreement of others in their tribe. With that decision, Lawyer and a few followers signed the new treaty which would reduce the Nez Perces lands by 75 percent. The remainder of the tribal leaders left the council to await a separate negotiation concerning their own holdings.

By blatant trickery typical of the Indian commissioners of the period, the white spokesman then gathered the signatures of Indians unqualified to speak for the tribe. Thus, they were able to return to Washington with the claim that all of the tribe—that is, a sufficient number of signatures—had agreed to the new treaty, and that "head chief" Lawyer had decreed the treaty to be in effect. Of the $262,500 which was to be paid for nearly a million acres of land, half was to be reserved for "Indian removal" of the Non-treaty bands into the reservation run by Chief Lawyer.

Joseph and the other Non-treaty chieftains were incensed when they learned of these claims and found that the whites had no further interest in individual negotiations with each of the bands. Joseph, an old man by now and nearly blind, tore up his copy of the treaty and in a deeply symbolic act burned the Bible which he had carried with him since his baptism nearly 30 years earlier. He declared before a council that he would have nothing more to do with the white men or their religion, and he retired with his band to the still untrammeled boundaries of the Wallowa. He died a few years later, a sickly and heartbroken man.

Joseph's young son laid the skin of his father's favorite horse on the covered grave. Thin poles, stripped of their bark and painted red, were planted around the grave. Two bells hung from these poles, gently tinkling in the slightest breeze. All had been done according to custom. Only then did Young Joseph, now Chief Joseph, become the full peace chief of his tribe. All eyes and minds

Smithsonian

Timothy, one of the Christian chiefs sympathetic to the whites.

turned toward him; for more troubles with white intruders were on the horizon.

For a few years before his father's death, and for some time afterwards, Young Chief Joseph was confronted with increasing tribal demands for something more than diplomacy with the whites. No white man had the right to infringe upon the lands of the Wallowa. Even within the white man's legal framework, the lands of Joseph's band had never been rightly sold. Yet another treaty had been demanded by the government in 1867 for the placement of several military outposts on the remaining Nez Perces lands. But this time, there had been no effort to engage the Non-treaty chieftains. Instead, Lawyer, Jason, and Timothy—the remaining loyal Christian leaders—were transported to Washington to put their signatures to the agreement for *all* the Nez Perces. Many more promises of money and facilities were made by the government, but this was the period of the corruption-bound Grant Administration, and only the signers among the Nez Perces realized any benefits from the agreement.

After a series of protests by the old chief, his son, and the Nez Perces agents, President Grant had been induced to sign an order putting the Wallowa lands in the public domain. But the majority of whites paid no heed to this requirement. Squatters by the dozens simply "settled" themselves where they saw fit. The "squatter game" had been learned well by the white intruders. The nomadic Nez Perces, now largely returned to their old way of life, moved their quarters frequently according to the seasons. And whenever they moved from one spot to another, nearby whites would simply enlarge the illegal holdings of the previous year and fence the new acreage. The Indians had no recourse; the Indian Bureau in Washington had come to be the most corrupt public office in the land, with missionaries and retired Army officers dividing reservation lands like a cake.

In some cases, a reservation agent—such as the new Nez Perces agent, John Monteith—had integrity and good intentions in handling the monies and facilities for a tribe. But even those like

*Timothy, Lawyer and Jason, the Indians who
negotiated the ineffective treaty of 1863.*

Monteith who stopped the swindling and tried to halt the squatters usually had the white Christian's penchant for fencing his Indians into a spiritual corral. Monteith, a gaunt, bearded, religious zealot, had no tolerance for the presence of worship of any religion but his own. He was also impatient with the Indian practices of buffalo hunting and camas gathering, because they caused the remaining Nez Perces farms to be neglected and because he thought the roaming life fostered a very un-Protestant leisure and laziness among the Indians.

As time passed, Monteith's Christian sense of love and charity and saving souls did not help him remain impartial towards these heathens with their disorderly ways. He went so far as to call out troops to watch the trails and stop the bands as they traveled toward buffalo country or the camas meadows. He made some successful efforts to stop the white encroachment on reservation lands, but he had no authority—and little sympathy—for the Non-treaty bands, so that the squatting and theft were flagrant in these areas.

Young Chief Joseph could not miss the growing anger in the faces of his tribesmen. At council after council, warriors and elders came forth to complain of appropriated lands or of unfair treatment by the white legal system which was supposed to protect them. By 1872, the white man's arrogance toward the Non-treaty bands had turned into open belligerence. Joseph, like his father, was both a man of peace and a realist. He knew that the Non-treaty bands were merely tolerated by the government and that any hostile actions by the Indians would be met by their forcible removal to the reservation or worse. He was therefore relentless in his efforts to curb the mounting wrath of his people. He rode everywhere, followed by his brother Ollokut, and by Bow-and-Arrow and Two-Flocks-on-Water, the three war chiefs of his tribe. Wherever he went, his great eloquence was aimed at the young warriors who were ready to die in battle to avenge a point of pride.

Joseph had a formidable task. By the mid-1870s, Monteith himself was protesting the injustices and string of atrocities com-

Indian agent Monteith had no tolerance for the worship of any religion but his own.

mitted by the whites against the Non-treaty Nez Perces in particular. Lynchings, rape, murder and mutilation were becoming commonplace, and neither the military nor the civil authorities were willing to antagonize the white settlers by punishing the criminals among them. The killing of Chief Eagle Robe was typical.

A white man named Ott, a squatter, had settled on a tract of land next to the garden of Eagle Robe, a much venerated chief who was retired and living alone in peace. While the old man was away on a visit to a nearby village, Ott extended his fence to include the chief's garden. When Eagle Robe returned and angrily tore the fences down, Ott casually drew his revolver and shot the old chief. It took all of Monteith's and Chief Joseph's influence to prevent retaliatory violence by Eagle Robe's son Wahlitis, who was one of the finest and most fierce young men of the tribe. They convinced the young warrior that Ott would be dealt with by the white authorities. Indeed, he was arrested, but his trial ended in an acquittal on the grounds of self-defense.

The continuing crisis came to a head in the summer of 1875. The governor of Oregon, campaigning for votes among the landless newcomers to his state, prevailed upon the authorities in Washington to rescind Grant's presidential order on the grounds that the Non-treaty Nez Perces had violated their claim to their lands by refusing to remain in one spot throughout the year. What the governor knew and most of his supporters did not was that the Wallowa was a wilderness made up mainly of roaring streams, rocky buttes and high-altitude timbered valleys wholly unsuitable for the covetous white farmers. The Christian Nez Perces, by then squeezed into an even smaller reserve and resentful of the freedom in the Wallowa, had joined the whites in campaigning against their tribesmen.

Monteith protested the new presidential order—he knew that it would provoke trouble—but the governor's arguments, and his backers, were more forceful in distant Washington. Joseph and his people were stunned by the order. And when Monteith came to the

Nez Perce life demanded a council for nearly any important event.

Wallowa council, asking the bands to avoid further difficulty by removing themselves to the reservation lands, the Indian leaders refused any further discussion with the treacherous whites. They would remain where they had been born.

Joseph attended one further meeting with the whites in 1877—a visiting commission called from Washington by Monteith and the new military commander General O. O. Howard—but the chief's condescension, his shrewd argument, and his stubborn refusal to compromise merely irritated the commissioners and convinced them that he was a troublemaker. They returned to Washington with no further recommendations for settling the dispute. Military force seemed the only alternative.

*Joseph and his people refused the white man's order
to abandon the Wallowa Valley, their ancestral home.*

3.

The "Righteous" War of the Christian General

AGENT Monteith had never approved of the independence of Joseph's band and the other Non-treaty Nez Perces. He was particularly exasperated with Joseph, whose cool logic and implicit contempt made all of the white demands seem not only unjust but "unchristian." Even so, Monteith had generally done what he could to fairly represent the Nez Perces cause and to protect the Indians, Christians and non-Christians, from further white abuses. He feared open warfare and made every effort to prevent it. Monteith became a changed man during that uncertain winter of 1877. Perhaps he was goaded by the envious Christian Indians in his charge. Perhaps his zealous missionary's soul could no longer bear the affront of the Non-treaty "heathens," who argued so fervently for a continuation of their lives away from Monteith's "righteous path." Perhaps he was worried about being replaced at the agency.

Whatever the motive, Monteith turned from his formerly peaceful methods and asked for the authority to call in the Army and force the non-Christian Nez Perces to enter, and remain in, the reservation at Lapwai. The man in charge of the Army, General Howard, the "Bible General," was in agreement with Monteith's determination to finally Christianize the heathens. On February 9, Monteith requested Joseph's presence at the Lapwai Agency to discuss the arrangements to be made concerning the forthcoming removal of the Non-treaty tribes to the reservation.

It was a brash and provocative action if for no other reason than that the mountains and passes between the Wallowa and Lapwai were still blocked by snow. The journey was slow and arduous, but Joseph came, with Ollokut and a few warriors. After a rest and the preliminary amenities, the tribal leaders met formally with Monteith and were struck speechless by his demand, in the form of a

Chief Joseph

sanctioned government order, that all of the Non-treaty tribes should be off their lands in the Wallowa by April 1.

Joseph was enraged, not by the order—it was expected, and they were largely resigned to it—but by the arrogance and stupidity of Monteith's deadline. Anyone who had lived in Nez Perces country for as long as Monteith knew very well that the rivers, swollen by melting snow, are mostly impassable at that time of year. Only the strongest animals in their large herds of horses and cattle could ever cross the Salmon or the Clearwater in the early spring. The calves and colts would surely be lost. And what of the elderly, the children, and the sickly among the tribes?

The argument went on for hours. The Indian leaders insisted from the outset that the deadline be extended until the end of the summer, when the rivers are low and easy to ford. Monteith and Howard remained adamant, and finally, the Indians agreed reluctantly to start moving by June. They knew, however, that even a June migration could mean a loss of half of their herds. They had agreed to Monteith's demand only in order to return to their winter quarters and to gain time for further bargaining.

As the peace leader and spokesman of the Non-treaty bands, Joseph was philosophically resigned to the eventual displacement of his people from their ancient homeland. He gravely promised the bands to continue his attempts to preserve the land where his father was buried. His best hope, however, was for an unhappy compromise with the whites. Joseph made it plain to the Nez Perces that they should begin to prepare themselves for the move north among the Christian tribes.

To Joseph, the grim alternatives—defiance and warfare—were unthinkable. The list of defeated neighboring tribes was long and well-known to the Nez Perces: the Sioux, Cheyenne, Mineconjou, Dakotas, Junkpapas, Brules and Gros-Ventres. Moreover, the Battle of Little Bighorn was but a year-old memory, and all of the Indians lived in fear of the tensions and bitterness left by the Custer massacre at the hands of the Sioux under Sitting Bull.

The Nez Perces bands heard Joseph's advice and began making plans to round up the herds. Despite the snow and the swollen streams, they hoped to gather as many of the animals as they could for fear that if they were to wait, they might be forced onto the reservation with their herds still at large. The young warriors were dispatched to undertake the almost impossible job of searching hundreds of miles of grazing lands scattered among the snow-covered mountains and glades. A "no-fight" order was reissued to them before they left.

Meanwhile, Joseph tried again to preserve the Wallowa. He asked for another council, this time with the general. Then, before the scheduled meeting, he fell ill, and sent Ollokut in his stead. The proud and impatient Ollokut endured days of hard riding through swollen streams and blocked mountain passes only to be met, not by General Howard but by an unconcerned young lieutenant by the name of Boyle. Boyle—patriotic and ambitious—was bitter about the severe defeats of the U.S. Army the previous year. He was also eager to demonstrate his iron-handed contempt for the "treacherous savages." He listened to the long speech of Ollokut, praised the Nez Perces' historically peaceable relations with the whites, and then reiterated the government's determination to transfer the five Non-treaty bands to the reservation. The Non-treaties were to move or be moved at gun point. Ollokut, no diplomat himself, left the meeting fuming and cursing Boyle as a "liar," the foulest insult in the Nez Perces' language.

Yet another council was called, this time with General Howard, and again Joseph was forced by ill health to send his brother. Ollokut presented a compromise drawn up by Joseph. The Umatillas, the Cayuses, and the Walla-Wallas would abandon their lands, which had already been largely claimed or confiscated by the whites, and would join the Nez Perces in the Wallowa and the Imnaha valleys. Howard did not accept this idea; it would involve too much paper work and red tape to change the plans of the earlier presidential commission. The commission map, in which the Wallowa had been omitted from Nez Perces territory, was put before Ollokut once again. In a fit of anger, he tore up the map.

A final grand council was set for May 3rd. All the Non-treaty chiefs were invited and most attended. An escort of 50 warriors, impeccably arrayed and all at least six feet tall, was gathered by Joseph to impress the white officers and government agents. The Indians elected the old philosopher-poet Too-Hool-Hool-Zute to speak for them after each chief had had his opportunity to make an opening statement. The proceedings were long and tedious by the white man's standards, and General Howard soon grew impatient and snappish.

From the very beginning, there was friction between the Bible General and Too-Hool; for each was a stubborn and intolerant spokesman for his own culture and point of view. After a three-day recess, the council became a personal battle between Howard and Too-Hool. Too-Hool was as arrogant and provocative in his way as the general. How is it, he asked repeatedly, that the white men professes Christian principles and the Ten Commandments, yet would take the Nez Perces lands with neither legal nor divine rights but merely fire-power? And from whence, he asked, comes this power of General Howard?

> God is the father of us all; the earth is the heritage of all men; and after all, who is General Howard in the vast dominion of God's creation? Has Howard created the mountains? Filled the rivers? Has he made the sun, the plains, the animals? What, indeed, really belongs to General Howard, who doesn't even know the Wallowa is Nez Perces land?

This direct attack infuriated the Bible General. He ordered his guards to put the irritating Too-Hool under house arrest, and the other chiefs agreed that Too-Hool should retire from the meeting without making further trouble. Joseph and White Bird were able to arrange his release two days later, with the promise that he would behave with more tact and not further endanger the Indians' case.

They might as well have let Too-Hool continue to vent his anger and frustration, for nothing was to be changed by this new council. The differences were irreconcilable. Monteith and Howard were eager to prove their resolve after the Custer disaster, and they thought it best finally to deal with the Nez Perces problem firmly

The proud warrior Ollokut had no patience
with the white man's negotiations.

and with dispatch. The Non-treaty bands were ordered to leave the Wallowa as soon as possible and no later than June 15.

By the middle of May, most of the Nez Perces herds had been gathered at various points near the juncture where the five bands were to meet before the final two-mile trek north to the reservation boundaries. The herdsmen had already lost hundreds of young animals. Gangs of white men also had a hand in diminishing the rich herds of the Non-treaty Indians. Knowing the plight of the Indians, many of the white settlers and prospectors had joined in the round-up themselves, gathering any strays they could find and sometimes deliberately stampeding and scattering herds already collected by the Indian scouts. The Indians, concerned for the safety of their families, were helpless against this subtle warfare by the local whites.

By the first week of June, the Indians' gathering place, an old camping ground called Tepahlewam, was overcrowded with the families, tepees and herds of the five evicted Non-treaty bands. Despite the forthcoming exile, there was calm and even an air of holiday in the camp. Relatives visited relatives after the winter's separation. Women were busy with the children, with gossip, and with the springtime tasks of digging and preparing camas and kouse roots or working on buffalo robes. The chiefs gathered at night councils and smoked their pipes. A large group of hunters had gone to the buffalo country and were due to return. The rest of the men tended the herds or repaired their tools and weapons.

It was a beautiful time in the Nez Perces lands. The meadows surrounding the camp at Tepahlewam were alive with color. Tall grasses filled the glades. The apple trees were sowing their white petals and delicate sweet aroma. The camas fields, extending for acres toward buttes and mountains, were an ocean of velvety-blue flowers rippling in the warm afternoon breezes.

The day came to move north, but only a handful of families headed toward the Lapwai Reservation. Agent Monteith sent a few of his Christian Indians to remind the Non-treaty tribes that it was time for them to leave the Wallowa. "Something might hap-

*A Nez **Perce** woman and her children in traditional dress.*

pen" if they weren't on their way soon. "We are ready," they answered, but they made no effort to move on. They understood that they *must* leave; they were fearful of the consequences of their defiance; yet they were compelled to delay. Every lovely summer dawn, the teepees were still up and the camp fires were burning brightly, sending thin trails of smoke into the air. No one would make the decision to move. No one could face the prospect of abandoning his ancient homeland.

A strange mood settled over the camp, a mood of careless resignation, of numb unreality. They reminisced under the warming sun: "A son was born here, a daughter was married there, a nephew killed his first deer beyond that butte." Many left camp briefly to pay respects to the tombs of their dead. Joseph and Ollokut had put two new red-striped poles and a fresh horsehide over their father's grave. The bands began to put great emphasis on the old customs and etiquette—working, visiting, trading, feasting—as if their familiar way of life was to continue unthreatened forever. The young warriors, particularly frustrated by the prospect of exile, passed the time painting their bodies, talking bravely, and making frequent war parades through the camps.

Joseph, in his respected role as peace chief, had managed to contain the prideful anger of the warriors to these symbolic displays of manhood, but the men were resentful nevertheless and might well have exploded into violence if Joseph had forced the issue and insisted that the tribes begin their journey into the reservation. As it was, Joseph, too, was paralyzed by the dilemma of his tribe. He believed the decisions of Monteith and the general to be unjust and ill-considered; he knew the confiscation of the Wallowa was an illegal act, even by the standards of the whites; he also knew that open defiance would mean the dashing of all hopes for redress and the destruction of his people. He knew that the tribes would have to comply eventually, but he could not—nor would any Nez Perce man—lead the bands into captivity.

Joseph, Ollokut, and a few friends left the camp on June 9th in order to slaughter several cattle for a promised feast *in memoriam*

A restless Nez Perce parades his beautiful horse through camp.

for a friend who had died the previous year. On June 12th, while his party was away, there was another of the noisy and posturing war parades. As the young braves passed through Joseph's camp, Wahlitis, one of the most impetuous of the men, inadvertantly led his horse over a patch of drying kouses as he was showing off for a pretty young woman. The middle-aged husband of the woman, jealous at the obvious admiration his wife bestowed on the handsome Wahlitis, angrily scolded the youth for his carelessness.

> See what you do? Playing brave you ride over my woman's hard-worked food. If you are so brave, why do you not go kill the white man who killed your father Eagle Robe?

The criticism stung Wahlitis. Ott, the murderer, was now farming Eagle Robe's lands and arrogantly driving away any Indians who passed nearby. The hurt of his father's death several years earlier was now healed, but at that moment, when the whole Nez Perces nation was to be humiliated, Wahlitis felt deeply the need to strike back—to avenge his father, to avenge his forefathers.

The following morning, Wahlitis, his friend Sarpsis, and Swan Necklace, a very young and inexperienced brave, left the camp. The latter had not been told what the three were to do; warriors would often take a young one along on a hunting trip, mainly to hold horses and perhaps to learn something. When the three had ridden through the night to the Ott farm, Swan Necklace was told of their mission. Wahlitis would reject Joseph's wisdom and take vengeance on the white man.

The farm was abandoned. Ott had fled when he heard that the Indians were being moved north to the reservation. He rightly feared retaliation. The two warriors were not satisfied; they were committed to a holy task. They knew of another nearby white man who had been cruel to the Indians, a man named Divine who had stolen all the land he owned and enjoyed setting his fierce dogs on the Nez Perces. Divine was at home, and when he saw the three braves, he ran inside, retrieved his gun, and began shooting at the intruders. Sarpsis nodded to Wahlitis and Wahlitis, given first privilege, killed Divine with one shot.

Wahlitis has started the war.

The bloodshed went down well. They continued on to the John Day ranch, to even the score with a cruel and foul-tempered man who was known for beating and abusing Indians. The warriors were unable to find Day in the farmhouse, but circling the area, they discovered two field workers who were brought down quickly by the warriors' bullets. Another enemy of the Indians, Henry Elfers, was killed, and a fourth white man escaped with a serious wound. The warriors then camped near the Nez Perces' gathering place and sent young Swan Necklace into the village to inform the elders and the chiefs of what they had done. Tell them, said Wahlitis, that we have started the war for them.

4.

A Rout at White Bird Canyon

WITHIN minutes of Swan Necklace's arrival and announcement, an excited warrior was riding throughout the camps shouting: It is war. The young ones have started war. He called out for volunteers for further forays against the whites who had most abused their people, and in a short time, a war party of 16 had been recruited and were riding with Wahlitis and Sarpsis. For three days, this small angry band of Nez Perces rampaged across the Salmon River Valley, killing and looting with specific vengeance in mind at first, and then, when they had got hold of whiskey, in a drunken frenzy of wanton violence. In the end, 15 white men had been killed, women and children were mistreated and terrorized, property was destroyed and plundered, and a woman and child were missing and presumed murdered. The white settlers were terrorized and outraged; the camp at Tepahlewam was shocked and fightened by the violence.

During the massacre, the elders and chiefs of the bands held council. Independence of decision-making was an important thing in Indian life during a crisis. They left each man to follow a path of his own choice, and many families took the opportunity to leave, either for the reservation or for the mountains. Chief Looking Glass and his people decided not to participate in the inevitable war. His followers and most of Joseph's Wallowa band moved their campsite a few miles away in the hope of avoiding any association with the marauders, most of them from the Salmon River group.

Chief White Bird, a well-known medicine man, and Chiefs Too-Hool-Hool-Zute and Hahtalekin preferred to prepare for a fight. They led their people to less open country, in White Bird Canyon. There they would wait to see what was ahead for them. No one of the Nez Perces' bands wished to remain at Tepahlewam and trust that a flag of truce or further councils would continue to placate the Army.

Joseph and Ollokut had been summoned by two worried tribesmen and arrived as the giant village at Tepahlewam was breaking up. Riding among the panicked bands, Joseph urged those present not to flee and warned that it would only prove their common guilt. He and his sound advice had come too late. The next morning, all that was left standing were the teepees of his family, those of Ollokut, and the immediate relatives of the two. The brothers consulted and decided to follow their tribesmen to White Bird Canyon.

It was the end of almost half a century of ceaseless work by their father and themselves for peace between the whites and the Nez Perces. Joseph was now resigned to war but fearful of the price this war would exact of his people in the weeks and months to come. As a diplomat and peace chief, he could no longer prevent the war, nor could he take a hand in conducting it to attain what he would consider the best for his people. According to Indian custom, he would be retained as a permanent advisor and would remain with the camp of women and children to take charge of their valuable herds of horses. The fighting would be planned and run by war leaders, such as his brother Ollokut, who had been selected by their fellow warriors.

Confusion reigned in the camp at White Bird Canyon. Despite the ritualistic war parades by the young men, no one among the Nez Perces had been prepared for warfare. Their escapist holiday mood had been abruptly stripped away by the reality of Wahlitis's atrocities and the certainty of reprisals by the white soldiers. While they no longer pretended that their problems did not exist, they had not yet had time to grasp the new, and far more dangerous, situation.

How would they fight a far larger and better armed troop of professional soldiers while encumbered with the women and children, the elderly, the precious herds of cattle and horses, and the exigencies of daily living? And even if they should defeat one white army, what then? There would be others to follow; the Nez Perces would not get back the Wallowa; nothing would be resolved; there

A fully-feathered War Chief carries a war pole for battle.

could be no Nez Perces victory. They would fight because of pride and intolerable frustration. They would fight because they must.

Experienced warriors finally took control of the situation. They repositioned the camp and the herds deep into the V-shaped canyon. Then the warriors moved forward into the narrow entrance to the canyon. They would use a classic Indian strategy, involving decoy and flanking movements. Sentinels were placed on distant buttes nearest the canyon portal. A sizeable group of warriors would provide the bait in a battle line midway along the V of the canyon. A small band of sharpshooters were scattered among the rocks along the canyon walls. Behind the riflemen, hidden in a ravine, Ollokut waited with a group of 50 mounted warriors. Joseph and White Bird had gathered the herds and remained in the rear with the rest of the Indian band. Joseph continued to insist on a suit for peace, and all of the war chiefs agreed that they would send a white flag of truce before any fighting began. However, they were now prepared for, and expected, the worst.

Nearly 100 soldiers, bolstered by a handful of civilian volunteers and 12 of the Christian Nez Perces as scouts, were sighted making camp shortly after midnight on the morning of June 17th. The call of the raven echoed across the night sky. The few veteran Indian fighters among the soldiers knew from the eerie calls that they had been detected. The inexperienced soldiers General Howard had sent on a forced march to White Bird Canyon were exhausted, nervous and far from eager after the Custer episode, to confront the storied Nez Perces warriors. Most of the enlisted men were Irish and German immigrants, recruited for an Army sojourn only in order to get to the Western frontier, where they might seek their fortunes. The officers, too, though professional soldiers, had had little experience and were further handicapped by their vague instructions "to see what's going on" and to bring the tribes into the reservation.

In the Nez Perces war camp, most of the warriors were preparing for battle by stripping to their breechcloths and painting their faces and bodies with a red ochre dye. Their bodies primed and painted for the fighting, their next concern was the spirit. They retired individually with their "wyakin" charms and amulets in order to chant their war and death chants. Each song, composed by the warrior himself, characterized his attitude toward life and the special quality of his spiritual guide. Some celebrated the universality of the life cycle, comparing themselves to

> the leaves of a tree
> the drops of the spring rain
> I have come from what I know not
> and there I shall return.

Others solemnly bowed low in a profound moment of spiritual communion with the sun, their father, and the earth, their mother.

The sun was barely casting its pale-gray morning light on the beautiful land when the soldiers reached the canyon. Six warriors, fully feathered and painted and carrying a white flag of truce, rode out to meet them. As the Indian truce party approached, one of the volunteers, a barroom hero named Chapman, fired. The battle followed at lightning speed.

In the first minutes, at least a dozen of the raw young soldiers dropped from their saddles, the victims of the sharpshooters on either side of the canyon. The teenaged bugler, Jimmy Jones, had been the first casualty, making the confusion among the unpracticed soldiers all the more difficult for the officers to control. As the Army pulled back in disarray, the forward line of warriors raced forward in a brutal attack which split the soldiers into small, disorganized platoons. At the head of the charging warriors were the three braves who came to be called "The Three Redcoats"; for they led the war charge while contemptuously waving red blankets to make themselves easy targets. Among the Redcoats was Wahlitis, eager to regain his reputation as a courageous warrior.

In the midst of the melee, a flanking movement was started by Ollokut and his 50 warriors. They thundered over the crest and onto the battleground, whooping and shooting from under the necks of their horses like an army of phantoms. A group of 18 soldiers cornered against a rock wall were brought down by the Indians in minutes. Another trumpeteer was killed; and before an hour was up, the superior forces of the U.S. Army were fleeing in utter panic and confusion. Behind them they left 34 dead. The Indians, who suffered only two wounded, had more than fulfilled their reputation as courageous fighters and exceedingly good marksmen.

The Nez Perces women scurried across the battleground, collecting arms, ammunition and any supplies or clothing they thought useful. No scalping or mutilating was allowed then or at any time during the war. (The same cannot be said for Howard's forces.) The most precious items the women gathered were 30 or 40 rifles. The Indians had had very few rifles, only one for every two men, and they were mainly old-fashioned muzzle-loaders, which had little value in such a war.

The defeat of the Army became electrifying news not merely in the West but across the nation. First the Custer massacre and now this. Settlers everywhere in the Northwest demanded immediate action. The press exaggerated the seriousness of the defeat, ignoring the Army's immense superiority in arms and personnel while building the Nez Perces warriors into a ferocious juggernaut. Howard's superiors ordered an immediate vindication of the Army, and he hurriedly called in reinforcements from all the Western outposts and from as far away as Alaska and Georgia. While he waited for a strengthening of his forces, he drilled his garrison relentlessly. In a week, he was ready to move again with a force of 500.

After the Nez Perces had celebrated their victory, they immediately prepared to move their camp; they knew General Howard would soon return to avenge the crushing defeat of his army. As to their next course of action, the Nez Perces were uncertain. The councils argued long into the night. Where should they go? South, north, east, west? There were white men everywhere; and there were many forts and soldiers as well, thanks to the Sioux uprising and the Custer defeat of the previous year.

Five Wounds and Rainbow, two of the most celebrated Nez Perces warriors, joined the councils after returning from buffalo country. They proposed a strategy which was immediately and unanimously adopted. The tribes would gain time by crossing the

*The soldiers fled the battleground at Whitebird Canyon
after their devastating defeat.*

swollen Salmon and waiting there for the white soldiers. Then as Howard's large and heavily equipped army struggled across the river, the Indians would recross the Salmon a few miles upstream, gaining several days on Howard. With this lead, they could head north, then northeast, through the most difficult terrain toward the buffalo country. There they would replenish supplies, rest themselves and their herds, and if Howard persisted, try to ally the nearby Crow to their cause. In the worst circumstances they could continue north to Canada, where they might join with the forces of Sitting Bull and his Sioux tribes.

The crossing of the treacherous Salmon began the following morning, even before the sun had risen. As when they had crossed the river enroute to Lapwai, the work was done swiftly and systematically. The tribe acted as a body—chiefs, warriors, women, the elderly, the children—everybody moved surely, patiently, efficiently in an amazing communion of purpose. First, the village was dismantled by the women while the young men gathered the vast herds of horses and cattle and drove them toward the river. Joseph himself supervised the crossing of their herds. He moved the younger and weaker animals into the center of the herd, then ran them for a distance before driving the galloping pack into the powerful current. Girdled by shouting riders and driven through the torrent by their own momentum, most of the thousands of animals successfully fought their way across to where other herders were waiting.

When the village was packed, the women turned to the quick manufacture of boats for the crossing. While some gathered the willow branches, others stood by the shore of the Salmon, weaving the branches and leather thongs into raft-like "bull-boats" covered by buffalo hides. The strong hides, hairy side up, protected the supplies and passengers (the children and elderly) as the boats were dragged across the river by ropes tied to the necks of two, three, or four strong ponies managed by a young man. Sometimes, two seasoned swimmers accompanied the boat and helped to hold it steady. At all times, the crossing was well-protected by scouts;

Nez Perce women broke camp and prepared for each move.

the best warriors on the best horses with the most accurate rifles had been posted in every direction.

Two days after the Indian families were safely across the Salmon, Howard and his troops appeared on the shore of the river. Under his command were 400 soldiers, 100 local volunteers, dozens of Crow scouts, tons of food and ammunition, two cannons, several Gatling guns, and not a single boat. The Indian strategists had counted on the Army's being heavily encumbered, forced like a snail to drag its shell wherever it goes.

A few shots were exchanged from either side of the Salmon, and James Reuben, a Christian Nez Perce with Howard's army, engaged in a hollering match with the rear guard of the fleeing tribe. You should give yourselves up, Reuben called. Return to the reservation. You are crazy. To which one of the warriors shouted back, We are not little boys like James Reuben, begging food from the agent, or selling our lands and brothers to fill our stomachs.

By the time General Howard had finally started crossing the river, losing dozens of mule packs, the Indians were already recrossing the Salmon and heading north. By twice moving a large group of people and animals across a raging river within the incredible span of 30 hours, they had gained a reliable four-day lead on General Howard.

Bull-boats, covered with buffalo hides, carried supplies
and passengers across the treacherous Salmon River.

5.

General Howard's "Gallant Charge"

LEAVING General Howard to his problem of twice fording the raging Salmon with his inexperienced troops and burdensome supply wagons, the canny Nez Perces moved northward toward the Clearwater River and the Weippe Prairie. Then with a four-day lead on the soldiers, the tribe camped for a time by the shores of the Clearwater. The secluded valley was an area well-suited for their herds, and its steep wooded hills also offered the Indians some natural shelter against the possibility of surprise attack. However, serious consideration of defenses and strategies of warfare were largely neglected by the Nez Perces. They showed no fear or urgency; they were reluctant to run or even to hurry away from Howard's army. They were oddly oblivious to the implications of the war that confronted them.

The Nez Perces had no direct experience with the relentless warfare of the whites. They knew only that the formidable army of General Howard had been soundly defeated at White Bird Canyon and then easily outmaneuvered at the Salmon River. In every subsequent skirmish between the soldiers and the rearguard of the Nez Perces, the Indians had succeeded in making the Army look foolish. For example, for almost two full days, a large group of soldiers were trapped and held tightly to the ground by a few Indian sharpshooters. All of the platoon's horses were taken and 13 soldiers were killed before the Indians finally became bored with the trench warfare and left the survivors to limp back to General Howard's camp. It is not surprising that the Nez Perces had begun to have absolute confidence in the "wyakin" powers of their warriors.

While the tribes rested alongside the Clearwater, Looking Glass and his band caught up with them and angrily reported the treachery of the white soldiers. Looking Glass had previously refused to participate in the war and had fled the Nez Perces encampment before it became a battleground. Nevertheless, because some of Looking Glass's young men had stayed to join in the hostilities, Howard had determined to punish the band. (It is more than likely that the general was also motivated by the fact that he needed a quick victory; and among all the Non-treaty Nez Perces, only Looking Glass and his band were even accessible.)

General Howard sent a small detachment of cavalry to Looking Glass's village under the command of Captain Whipple. Whipple dispersed his troops in a forest near the camp and then rode in with an escort to demand the chief's surrender. Taken by surprise, Looking Glass disclaimed any belligerency. But even at the moment the two men were talking, Whipple's troops were assembling for an attack. The chief's suspicions were aroused by sounds from the woods, and just as he turned from Whipple to call out a warning to his village, the soldiers charged.

The Indian losses were few—a boy of 17, and a young woman who drowned with her baby as she tried to flee across the river. The rest of the band managed to escape into the woods. Nevertheless, Looking Glass was outraged, and his speech to his compatriots at Clearwater was eloquent in its passionate call to arms:

> The white captain talked of peace even as the bullets of his soldiers began to fall upon our village like clouds of summer flies. For the women and the old ones it was very bad. We fought as well as we could and then we ran away, leaving everything behind us. The white soldiers pierced everything with their long knives. They burned everything. They trampled the gardens of vegetables and melons and cut all the young apple trees we planted some time ago. I tell you, my brothers, they acted like mad dogs. It is for this that I am here among you, now ready to fight the white soldiers. I will not forget this day.

Looking Glass's band was greeted generously by the other fugitive Nez Perces. They were given buffalo hides to make new teepees, and clothing, kettles and other supplies were provided from the booty at White Bird Canyon. There was no sign of Howard and his troops, so the Indians felt safe in passing a few more days gathering food and enjoying idle pursuits. Except for the roaming scouts and the warriors stripped for war, a stranger coming to the encampment during this time would have thought it a normal Indian village under the most peaceful conditions.

At one of numerous councils held during those days, the tribal elders and warriors decided that Looking Glass would take over as commander-in-chief. He had won the support of the other bands with his proposal that they proceed northward into Crow country. The Nez Perces had helped the Crows defeat the Sioux some years ago, so there was a strong conviction that the Crows would offer the Nez Perces asylum and perhaps even join in a united effort against the white general. The Nez Perces were at their greatest strength in that period, with about 140 warriors, an additional 50 men who did not or could not fight, and about 450 women and children.

The confidence and carelessness of the Nez Perces were increased to even greater heights of unreality when a small band of scouts led by Ollokut attacked 80 citizen volunteers. The skillful warriors pinned the white troop on a hilltop for an entire night and, at the same time, rescued a number of horses which had been stolen several days earlier in the attack on Looking Glass's village. The Nez Perces were invincible. They would proceed away from the cannons of General Howard at their own pace and with great pride. And when they were securely in Crow territory, the Great Father in Washington would see the courage of the Nez Perces and the error of his general's harassment of the tribe.

The Indians' pipe dream was burst at midday on July 11, only three weeks after their successful encounter with Howard's army at White Bird canyon. The tribe was, as usual for the Clearwater encampment, preoccupied with a variety of daily activities—none of them connected with the danger of a sudden attack by one of General Howard's commands. Several of the young men were racing horses along the river, others were bathing, and most were simply passing time in the warm sun. A cannon shot cast an

The simplicity of the Nez Perce home made it extremely mobile.

abrupt and absolute spell of silence over the camp. Then there was pandemonium as the Indians saw Howard and his troops rising over the distant rim of the river valley.

The Indian camp had been accidently stumbled upon by one of Howard's scouts, who had literally been "looking at the scenery" when he came to a high ridge and spotted the horse-racing along the riverbank. Most of Howard's army had already bypassed the Indian camp and was headed northward with no indication of where they might find the Nez Perces. When the wandering scout informed his commander, Howard turned his troops around and raced them southward toward the camp. He also deployed his artillery—a howitzer and two Gatling guns—to the ridge and began firing on the camp several minutes before his cavalry would be in a position to charge. Howard's command was now at full strength—about 400 fighting men plus another 200 scouts and supply troops. With the numerical advantage that Howard knew he held over the Nez Perces, he was very anxious to engage the Indians in a face-to-face battle.

In the camp, the warriors were arming themselves and rushing for their horses while the women waved blankets and shouted warnings. Old Too-Hool was the first of the warriors to ride to the defense of the village. To the chatter of the Gatling guns and the roar of the cannon, the chief led 24 of the best sharpshooters up the slope and to the head of a small ravine across the line of Howard's charge toward the village. This small and courageous band managed to pin down the long, awkward line of soldiers until the frustrated Howard ordered a halt and had his troop entrench for the night.

By that time, more warriors had joined Too-Hool's band, and to the surprise of the Army strategists, the Indians fortified their positions with boulders and barricades and then waited for the soldiers to charge their hilltop position. Sporadic skirmishing continued into the night, but the Army made no grand charges. To do so, Howard and his officers knew, would be a slaughter if the Nez Perces had even half of the hundred upon hundreds of warriors that rumor had granted them.

The women handled the move of the household.

At the moment of the Army's appearance, Chief Joseph, who remained in charge of the tribe's welfare and security, took immediate steps to ensure the safety of the women and children, the Nez Perces herds, and the tribe's possessions and supplies. While Too-Hool engaged the soldiers, the camp began to disperse across the river and into the woods. By the following morning, most of the warriors had joined their families, and only a small force of about 50 men remained to protect the tribe's retreat. Howard quickly broke through this rear guard, which easily slipped away and joined the fleeing tribe along the rugged Lolo Trail into the mountains to the north.

There was virtually no resistance and no equipment of importance when the Army finally took the abandoned Indian village. Indeed, the Indians had not only managed to stop the Army and then make a clean escape with a mere third of the casualties; they had also walked away with several thousand rounds of captured ammunition. General Howard's report to his superiors adopted a more optimistic view of the events: "Our troops bravely sustained the fire of the hostiles for two days," he wrote, ending his report with the reflection, "Finally, in a gallant charge, our men overtook the Indian positions, smashed their defenses and took possession of tons of goods and many horses." He also reported a huge number of casualties among his foes, an outright lie; and he failed to mention that every one of the "many horses" captured were sick or lame.

General Howard had clearly come to the realization that he faced a formidable adversary and that his reputation and career were now at stake.

Nez Perce weapons.

6.

The Great Retreat along the Lolo Trail

PROVIDENCE was smiling upon the Christian General; for at a time when the Nez Perces had eluded him for the second time and his reputation in Washington was sinking rapidly, two small bands of Nez Perces walked into captivity without a shot being fired on either side. One of the bands, 17 braves and some 30 women and children, led by Chief Red Heart, was returning from the buffalo country when they crossed paths with Looking Glass and the retreating tribes. Red Heart was unaware of the war which had begun in his absence, but he refused the invitation to join with his cousins, saying he had no quarrel with the white men.

Looking Glass tried to explain that he himself had wanted no part of war and yet had had his village completely destroyed by the Army. However, the old chief would not be warned. He pointed to his very small band: I have 17 men. Only 10 good warriors, three rifles. The rest are women and children. What would the white men want with these people of mine? What harm can we possibly do to them?

Chief Three Feathers, who had been a part of the war councils since White Bird Canyon, found the words of Red Heart convincing and announced to the tribe that he and a few followers would join with Chief Red Heart and return to the Kamiah. He was weary of the disruption and the threat of much bloodshed. Like Chief Joseph, Three Feathers questioned the sense of fighting a war over territory which the Indians were now abandoning to the white settlers and their army. Why not return to the Wallowa and try again to negotiate—or, if necessary, defend to the death the sacred land of their fathers? Unlike Joseph, Three Feathers and his tiny band felt more loyalty to their own convictions and security than to the wishes and well-being of the tribe as a whole. Joseph would stay and do his best to secure the women, the children and the

*Kamiah, where the tribe crossed the Clearwater
to begin their march along the Lolo Trail.*

possessions of his tribesmen; Three Feathers and Red Heart would return to the Nez Perces homeland.

The two dissenting bands left; the rest of the tribe continued northward in their forced march along the Lolo Trail. The following day the tribe heard from their rearguard the fate of Chief Red Heart and Chief Three Feathers. A detachment of Howard's cavalry met the Indians on the prairie, took them without discussion, stripped them of their horses and baggage, and forced them to walk the 60 miles nonstop to Fort Lapwai. They were considered prisoners of war and treated as such. Howard quickly identified the captives as hostiles taken at the Battle of Clearwater and thereby further colored the "success" of his campaign against the Nez Perces. He shipped the peaceable band off to a damp prison at Fort Vancouver while the newspapers across the country crowed about his great victory.

The Lolo Trail, one of the oldest and most rugged trails in the northwest, was chosen by the Indians as the safest exit to the north. They had to put time between themselves and Howard's troops, and they knew no better way than a rough overland passage. The Lolo was almost impossible to travel. It was steep and heavily timbered; there was almost no grazing ground for the horses; and the rocks, slippery mud, fallen timber and thick underbrush made every foot of the way a torturous and hazardous prospect. To pass along this trail, and to do so quickly, the Indians called upon all of their knowledge and skill both in woodlore (an ability they shared with other tribes) and in organization (a special aptitude of the Nez Perces).

A small advance guard under the command of Joseph was given the task of clearing the trail of fallen timber and large rocks. They were followed by young women who cleaned the narrow path of branches and made it readily passable for the tribe. The elderly shepherded the large herd of horses after the tribe had passed through. A heavy rearguard then followed up, replacing every log and branch and rock on the trail and adding many more until the path was virtually impassable once again.

Everyone worked with a minimum of authority or supervision;

everyone stoically endured the long forced marches to find adequate pasture for the animals. Their pace was incredible for a group of 600 people and more than 2,000 horses and cattle. While the soldiers pursuing them complained of exhausting and dispiriting 16-mile days, the Nez Perces managed to stay well ahead of the Army and eventually had a three-day lead. The daring flight began to take its toll, however. The soldiers reported numerous dead and brokendown Indian ponies along the trail.

General Howard had no hope of overtaking the Indians so long as they could select the trails they would follow. However, he had a secret weapon at his disposal which the Indians could never have anticipated. He used the newly strung wires of the telegraph to notify commands all over Montana and Idaho of the progress of the Nez Perces and of his desire to cut them off and trap them at the end of the Lolo Trail.

The nearest troops were a small contingent at work on the construction of Fort Missoula. The commander of the 30 soldiers, Captain Charles Rawn, combined his small troop with a group of 200 citizen-volunteers from the area, and the makeshift army erected a fortified line of defense across the canyon at the end of the Lolo Trail. The settlers in the area were near panic. Newspaper-inspired tales of atrocities and ruthlessness had preceded the Nez Perces, and both the small Army detachment and the citizen-soldiers expected to be faced with a fight-or-die situation—that hordes of fierce Nez Perces would soon sweep across the land, leaving nothing living in their path.

When the tribe finally appeared, exhausted and rather straggly after the ordeal of the trail, they found a small group of whites building breastworks and stone fortifications across the path. Joseph, Looking Glass, Ollokut, and a few other warriors assessed the situation and then decided to try to negotiate the matter. They had no quarrel with these people. Looking Glass ordered up a flag of truce and Captain Rawn came to talk things over with the Indians. The point of the discussion was brief and simple: The Nez Perces did not want to fight anybody; they simply sought to cross the Bitterroots and continue peacefully to buffalo country. It was their understanding that if they crossed the trail they would no longer be subjected to the laws of Idaho and General Howard would have to give up the pursuit.

Being a military man, Captain Rawn could not agree to the unheeded passage of the Indians. His orders were stop them. Nevertheless, the Nez Perces' reputation as fighters convinced him that he should not reject their request out of hand. The citizen-soldiers, in particular, had misgivings about demonstrating their bravery, especially now that they knew that the Indians had peaceful intentions. Both sides parted to discuss the issue overnight. During the night, however, the Indians found a way to bypass the breastworks. They decided, therefore, to pass through, even if the Captain rejected their safe passage and began firing.

In the white encampment, the volunteers deserted Captain Rawn by the dozens, until only about 30 were left to help the 35 soldiers from Fort Missoula. The civilians reasoned that resistance might well mean the destruction of their farms even if their lives were spared. If the Indians wanted peace and simply meant to pass through, let them. With his reduced troop, Captain Rawn, too, decided that discretion was the better part of valor. He remained in his tent the next morning, as the Indians moved out and bypassed the breastworks by edging along the timberline.

Descending into the Bitterroot Valley, the Indians journeyed in a different frame of mind. Most of them believed that their peaceful accommodation with Captain Rawn was a sign of renewed friendship between the Nez Perces and the whites. Wasn't it proof that the people of Montana would welcome them? Drawing a parallel with their own tribal laws regarding boundaries, they deduced that General Howard had no further authority.

Some of the warriors, Ollokut among them, were skeptical. They could not believe that it would end so easily and simply. They were restless and wanted to keep moving at a much faster pace than Looking Glass had set. Joseph remained neutral on the question as it was argued night after night at the council meetings. He still opposed both the fighting and the flight. He was in favor of surrendering to Howard in exchange for a guarantee that they might

Smithsonian

Looking Glass was chosen to lead the tribe across the Bitterroots.

retain a part of their homeland. Nevertheless, Looking Glass had been chosen commander of the journey, and most of the people believed that the war had ended. They were too happy; Joseph could not cast gloom upon their cheerful days. He reminded the other chiefs that Looking Glass had been chosen to lead. They owed him their loyalty at least until his plan was no longer successful.

With the threat of Howard seemingly behind them, the Indians moved very little in the next two weeks. They luxuriated in the green meadows and took much time restoring their horses to top condition. The settlers in the area were agreeable (if, indeed, they had any real choice in the matter), so the Nez Perces also engaged in considerable trading—buying rifles, ammunition and food stuffs, usually in exchange for one of the horses. Now and then, an incident occurred among the whites, but it was Looking Glass's mission to see that the tribe passed through the area peaceably and with propriety. When three of Too-Hool's men took food from a ranch, the chief insisted that they take three horses from the Indian herds to the ranch and brand them in the name of the rancher.

During this period of a rather sauntering pace toward Yellowstone and the plains of the Crow, a half-breed by the name of Poker Joe, also known as Lean Elk, joined the tribe. He and his band of traders had been summering in the Bitterroot Valley. He knew all the shortcuts to the buffalo country, and he volunteered his leadership as a guide. He also told the chiefs and elders that they should stop moving to buffalo country as though they were on a pleasure trip. He had had many dealings with the whites and with the U.S. Army. He knew that the Army did not dismiss its responsibilities so readily.

A young warrior, Lone Bird, affirmed Poker Joe's warning. The tribe had traveled very little in the past ten or twelve days, he noted. At their usual pace of 30 to 50 miles a day, the Nez Perces might have escaped to Canada. They had left the Lolo Trail and Captain Rawn on July 25; yet here they were August 7th and 8th, still in the valley, meandering toward the Crow country as if they had no worries in the world.

A rumor went about the camp after that more discouraging

The Nez Perce traded their valuable horses for food and ammunition.

council meeting. Wahlitis, the man who had started the war, told his friends and his wife that he had had a vision of his imminent death. Hearing this, the elders took note; the Nez Perces held great respect for a man's dreams. Looking Glass rode to a well-known medicine tree, where the horn of a Big Horn had been implanted with the point jutting outward. There, he made offerings to assure the success of his journey.

The chief had good reason to make his offerings. The telegraph chattered daily reports on the direction and activity of the tribe. General Howard demanded that the Indians be engaged, and he had sent 140 troops under the command of Colonel Gibbons to overtake and destroy the Nez Perces. Using forced marches and hired farm wagons to make speed, Gibbons rapidly gained on the tribe even after they had begun to follow Poker Joe's advice and were averaging 15 or more miles per day. Gibbons' troop also picked up reinforcements all along the route, including Captain Rawn's small force and a number of the settlers who had traded with the Indians in the Bitterroot Valley. A large group of Indian scouts also swelled Gibbons' army in the hopes of stealing horses from the Nez Perces.

This troop, now nearly 200 strong, caught up with the unsuspecting Indians while they were camped in the Big Hole Valley. Hidden in the darkness of the timbered hills above the tribe, Colonel Gibbons and his men waited tensely for the first glimmer of dawn.

7.

Slaughter at Big Hole Valley

THE exaggerated optimism which prevailed while the Nez
Perces traveled through the Bitterroot Valley had put them off
their guard. They hadn't posted a single scout in any direction,
and they had camped in a most vulnerable part of the Big Hole
Valley, even neglecting to ford Ruby Creek and to camp on the
opposite bank, where they would be protected from the full force
of a cavalry charge. While Colonel Gibbons and some 200 men
were watching and waiting beyond the hill ridges right above the
camp itself, the unsuspecting and careless Indians were passing
the evening in an almost holiday spirit.

The Army troops observed the whole life of the village from their
position. The sweet smell of the camas bulbs, steaming in their
earthen pits, wafted up from the valley and into the Army em-
placement. In the dusky light, the soldiers could see women
carving lodge poles, children playing tag, and clusters of men
gambling or talking. The veteran Indian fighters advising Colonel
Gibbons remarked again and again on how unusual it was to be at
such a close range and not be detected by scouts.

After observing the glories of a brilliant sunset streaked with a
single ribbon of delicate yellow, the Nez Perces village finally
ceased all activity and its denizens slept quietly under a calm,
cloudless sky. By the morning, even before the sun rose, the air
and sky had melded into a damp greyish tone that made the forms
of trees and hills and teepees barely discernible. Colonel Gibbons
readied his men at the ridge, and they waited in tense silence for
the first rays of dawn and the order to advance. They could dis-
tinctly hear whispers from below as a few Nez Perces women had
emerged from their buffalo robes to put wood on the embers of last
night's fires. The scent of fir trees was heavy in the damp predawn

air. A few dogs barked, and the tribe's herds, far to the right of Colonel Gibbon's central vantage point, began to stir.

As the sun appeared, an elderly Indian riding out to tend the herds, was suddenly confronted with the frightful vision of an advancing army stretched across the slopes above his village. He turned about and rode but a few dozen yards before a rifle shot thrust him from his horse. The shot echoed against the surrounding hills and wrenched the peaceful valley into a maelstrom of noise and terror.

Colonel Gibbons sounded the charge, and his troops responded, first with loud shouts of relief to be in action, and then with the wild throaty calls of a pack on the scent of blood. The first gun shot was followed immediately by a continuous crackle of rifle fire from the attacking soldiers. Then the cries and screams began as the groggy, half-naked Indians ran from their teepees to be cut down by the barrage of bullets.

The slaughter went along at an incredible pace. The Army was savage, shooting and bayonetting women and children indiscriminately, putting the village to the torch without concern for the old, the wounded and the small children who were trapped inside the burning teepees. The dead began to litter the village; heart-rending cries of death and pain filled the valley. A newborn child had his head smashed under the heel of a soldier. Another infant was left shrieking at his dead mother's breast, his tiny arm nearly severed by a bullet. Many of the women were shot down by Gatling guns as they ran with their children in their arms toward the river.

Some of the warriors had reacted quickly enough to escape across the river with their rifles. They immediately started firing back with their usual accuracy, and within 30 fast minutes of battle, the Indians had begun to reverse the offensive. Another group of warriors clustered in the upper part of the village were somehow holding their own ground, fighting both with rifles and by hand. Within an hour, the soldiers had lost complete control of the situation. The Indians in the upper part of the village were pushing the soldiers back toward the river.

From beyond the river, on a butte, a line of Indian sharpshooters set their marks on the officers and picked off 14 of the 17 assigned to the troop. By afternoon, the Indian vise had closed, and the soldiers, again abandoned by most of the citizen-soldiers and their assortment of Indian allies, were pinned against a hillside, without food, horses, water, or sufficient ammunition. Thirty-one enlisted men were dead, and 40 more had fallen with serious wounds.

As the warriors began building quick fortifications from which to watch the cornered soldiers, the surviving tribesmen gradually drifted back to their village to look for the missing and to attend to the casualties. The dead were laid on the ground near their tee-pees, where the women cleaned and dressed them for mourning and burial. Those few warriors who counted no deaths in the family were assigned to keep the soldiers pinned down. The others —stunned, exhausted, many of them wounded—moved silently from teepee to teepee, identifying the charred bodies, recovering belongings, aiding the wounded, searching for their families. Jo-seph, with Too-Hool and White Bird, worked for hours, organizing the shattered tribe, calling names for the missing and taking corpses to their families.

The casualties were staggering for the small tribe. Fifty women and children and nearly 30 warriors had been killed in the less than two hours that the Army was attacking. Wahlitis, one of the Three Redcoats, was dead. Others reported that his wife had grabbed her husband's rifle and killed the officer who had gunned down her husband, then was shot herself. Sarpsis, another member of the colorful Three Redcoats, had been killed. Ollokut's wife had been dangerously wounded and was lying in Joseph's teepee, while Ollokut led the warriors who were keeping the soldiers at bay. Rainbow was dead, and his inseparable companion Five Wounds vowed to die himself before the sun had set. As dusk approached, he walked, firing rapidly, straight toward the Army position and was finally felled a few yards from the barricades.

The evening brought a chilling scene. The Indians mourned loudly by the light of many fires, the chant for the dead rising into the darkness in pursuit of departing souls. One after another, the bodies were secretly buried, each warrior taking care of his own family and relatives, then cutting his hair shoulder-length to mark a death in the family. In the soldiers' outpost, too, there were cries from the wounded and the frightened. And over the whole valley, there was a tangible pall of shock and horror.

As the mourning subsided and settled into shock, Joseph rallied the tribe to begin moving the camp to the hills before Army reinforcements could fall upon them. The shattered village departed in small, silent, hesitant groups to a place called Takseen, or "Willows," near the Camas Meadows. The marshy spot, had for centuries, been frequented by the Nez Perces, who had gathered the thin willow branches growing there to make the baskets, hats, and pouches for which they were famous among all the tribes of the region. This nightmarish night, there was no industry among the women, no shouts of joyful greeting to a storied place of many happy memories. No one cared to erect a teepee. They set out robes and skins on the tall, damp grass.

Joseph prowled the campsite all the night, moving from family to family to calm them, to confer with the chiefs and elders, to gently reassure the sick and the wounded. A few more died of their wounds at Takseen, including the infant with the shattered arm and Ollokut's wife, Fair Lands. Joseph had the sad duty of burying his brother's wife, since Ollokut was back at Big Hole Valley commanding the warriors who were still holding the soldiers behind their stone and wood barricades. The tired and disheartened warriors shot at any Army movements behind the moonlit barricades, but they had no spirit for battle or even for revenge. They made no attempt to attack and destroy the troops. They wanted only to return to the remnants of their families, to chant over their dead and dying and to hold the suffering survivors near to them. Something precious—pride, perhaps, and a kind of innocence, and certainly any hope for victory—had been lost inexorably to the Nez Perces warriors.

One by one, the disheartened warriors asked to leave the watch over the "baby-soldiers," as they called the inexperienced Army

A surprise attack at this point in the Big Hole Valley
shattered the small Nez Perce tribe.

troops, and to join their families at Takseen. Ollokut permitted all but a few men to go, so that when the sun rose again, no more than a dozen braves remained to pin down nearly 100 soldiers. Shortly after the beautiful dawn sky had dimmed, a small detachment of cavalry and a pack train approached the barricades. The remaining handful of Indians rode away, firing the traditional two shots of contempt and farewell into the air. The white officers repaid the dignity and courage of the Nez Perces by permitting their Bannocks scouts to desecrate the fresh Nez Perces graves and the corpses. The Nez Perces finally understood the truth about war with the white men.

*Colonel Gibbons troops withdrew to shelter behind these trees
after their surprise attack had been repulsed.*

Rifle pits used by the soldiers in the Big Hole battle.

8.

The Strategy of Poker Joe

THE Nez Perce bands rushed blindly into the difficult terrain to the south in the hope of slowing their pursuers. They meandered aimlessly back and forth along the Continental Divide; their leaders still stunned by the suddenness and viciousness of the white attack. Finally, they paused one night, slowing the pace to allow the chiefs and elders to meet and discuss the strategy. The guidance of Chief Looking Glass was now in disrepute. The poor chieftain, dumbfounded by the losses to his tribe, rode silently alongside the warriors, his pride and confidence irreparably damaged. The facts were clear to the others; he had led them into a catastrophe. He would not lead them any longer.

Nearly everyone voiced an opinion at the council. Chief Looking Glass still held vague hopes that the Crows would come to the aid of the Nez Perces. The warriors pointed out that, thus far, other Indian tribes had been enlisted to fight against them, not with them. Poker Joe reiterated that their only chance of survival was to go to the territory of Sitting Bull in Canada. That great war chief lived more or less in peace under the jurisdiction of the Queen and the Royal Canadian Mounted Police. The Mounties, to most of the northern Indian tribes, had come to represent the embodiment of incorruptible justice and integrity.

Poker Joe assured the bands that they would be safe in Canada and that they could then recover their strength and balance while petitioning the American leadership for a more equitable solution to their territorial dispute. After several hours of discussion, the tribal leaders agreed that they had to escape the dogged pursuit of Howard as quickly as possible. The general had caught up with them in the Bitterroot Valley only because they had wasted too many days with a leisurely pace and an easy route. Once more,

An old cannon captured by the Indians at Big Hole.

they had to take the hardest path in order to complicate the advance of the soldiers.

Poker Joe had already proposed the route. They would first cross the Divide and the primitive Yellowstone country to the east, and then race directly north through the rolling Crow territory toward the Missouri River and the Canadian border. The eccentric Indian leader also suggested a new and unfamiliar strategy to the Nez Perces. He had gained his nickname from the whites, with whom he had drunk and gambled as a young man. He knew their thinking, their attitudes toward the Indians and toward warfare. He urged his tribesmen to recognize all white men as their enemy—to make war not merely against Howard and his troops, but against all the whites and all the Indian allies who would give aid to the Christian General in his relentless pursuit. He proposed a "scorched-earth" policy as the Nez Perces proceeded northward to Canada.

Poker Joe was unanimously voted commander of the tribe. The warriors knew him as a shrewd man and a cool one. They knew that he understood the whites better than anyone else among them. They also knew that their old ways were ineffective, that this self-confident renegade leader might be their only hope. Poker Joe agreed to lead, but only if the tribesmen met his conditions without question. Such an arrangement was counter to the Nez Perces philosophy, but Joseph and Ollokut strongly supported the cunning strategy of Poker Joe and the other leaders quickly relinquished their independence.

Poker Joe's first decree concerned the pace of their retreat. To gain distance over Howard's troops, who were then less than a day away, he ordered that the tribes would march from sunrise until mid-morning, rest while the sun was overhead, and then be on the move again until dusk had dimmed into blackness. There would be no stopping for any reason whatsoever, except at the appointed times.

His second decree was that five scouting parties, made up of three to ten warriors, would ride separately from the main group. These war parties would keep watch over the tribes and the herds.

They would skirmish with the Army whenever they had the opportunity. And they would systematically destroy or drive away everything living along the route behind them. No mercy would be given anyone, soldier or civilian. All horses would be taken; all livestock and game were to be wiped out or frightened away. Farms, stores of food, and fields would be destroyed. Wells and other water supplies would be spoiled.

The warriors began their new strategy the following morning. At the Montague Ranch, one group of scouts killed four men, took all the available horses, ransacked the house, and collected or destroyed all of its food stores. Another group of scouts swooped down on a cabin owned by two men, Meyers and Cooper. Cooper escaped, but the Indians killed Meyers and gathered all the food and horses for their families. The largest scouting group stopped a commercial wagon train headed for Idaho on its regular route from east to west. All but one of the drivers were killed (he escaped with two Chinese workers, who were spared by the Indians because they were unaccustomed to seeing men of their race). The scouts herded all the horses, ransacked the train, and then, finding whiskey, became involved in a drunken brawl in which one of them was mortally wounded.

The main body of the tribe moved at an incredibly fast pace. An old, wounded woman, sensing that she could never keep up with the new pace of the march, asked to be left behind. Her relatives argued with her for a time, but all realized that the survival of the tribe was primary. She accepted a little food and some water, then seated and singing a death chant, she watched the tribe disappear into the rolling hills.

Another of the tribe's elders, a respected medicine man named Kapoochas, also asked to be abandoned. When Lewis and Clark had first come to "visit" his people, Kapoochas had been in the prime of his life. He had seen the great Nez Perces tribe reduced to this desperate ragtag retreat from the whites, who had once claimed only friendship and the opportunity to introduce the "true God" to his people. Now Kapoochas insisted that he could bear no more of the suffering and sad fate of his tribesmen. He mounted a hillock and sat to await General Howard. He would die as a brave, defending his people against their mortal enemy. The rear scouts left him behind, knowing full well that the Old Father would be killed cruelly and scalped by the Bannock scouts in advance of Howard's army.

Just before entering the Yellowstone wilderness. Ollokut and 50 of his young warriors headed back toward the Army encampment at Camas Meadows. The tribe hoped to gain as much time as possible on their pursuers, and the strategy agreed upon was to take all of the Army horses in a night raid. The warriors rode swiftly and stopped at sunset just a few miles away from the soldiers' camp. There was none of the demonstration common to Indians prior to a battle—no parades, no gaudy paints, no sacred death chant by each warrior. The weary braves waited silently, quietly smoking their pipes and watching a beautiful summer day come to an end. They had been almost two months on the run and in battle. They had all lost a loved one at Big Hole—a wife, a parent, a cousin, brother or child. They had seen nearly half of their brother warriors fall before the enemy raid. There was no longer any honor in war with the white men. Many were coming to Joseph's view that there was little sense, and no hope, in their struggle.

The night was moonlit, unfortunate for a raid. But the warriors were optimistic. Black Hair, one of the warriors, had had a vision the previous night in which he saw horses running into the darkness. After the bugler's taps, when the soldiers' camp became fairly quiet, ten of the warriors crept into the camp to cut the horses and mules loose. The plan was that when the animals had been freed, the rest of the warriors would whoop down upon the camp and drive the herd away.

The few men silently penetrated the heavily guarded camp and began to release the pack animals, first cutting the warning bell that hung around each animal's neck. Hidden not far away, the other warriors waited for the gun shot which would signal that the hobbles were untied and the pickets removed. The shot came, but too soon and not from the Indians who were freeing the horses and mules. A warrior called Otskai, who was well-known for his lack of patience and good judgment, had again ruined a careful strategy.

With the warning shot, Ollokot had no choice; he ordered the charge into the Army herds. Shouting, waving blankets, occasionally shooting into the air, the Indians did their best to stampede the horses. But the first group had not had time to free many of the carefully picketed cavalry horses, so the effects of the raid were disappointing for the Indians. They drove away most of the mules with the cavalry in hot pursuit, and then lost several of the animals in a brief skirmish with the soldiers. In the course of the fight, the troops were once again easily flanked by the Nez Perces and one enlisted man was killed, several more were wounded. The Indians suffered no losses, and they succeeded in at least slowing down Howard for a few days.

The Indians camped that night by the shore of Henry Lake and enjoyed the first pleasant evening since the horrors of Big Hole. While on the run from Howard's troops, they had kept cooking to a minimum. The usual meal was primarily boiled salmon and whatever roots they could pick up along the way. But that night, they had stopped earlier than usual in order to allow the raiders to catch up with the main body of the tribe. Therefore, some of the small warrior groups were able to hunt and bring back large numbers of birds from the marshes surrounding the lake. At sunset, the view from the edge of the lake was magnificent. The lake swarmed with hundreds of white birds—geese, cranes, pelicans, swans—floating, diving, winging gracefully into the air.

Joseph and a few of the other chiefs had asked Poker Joe whether the tribe might stay on at the lake for a full day of rest. Certainly, they all needed it and they all felt more secure since the raid on Howard's camp. Poker Joe remained inflexible, almost to the point of antagonism. His answer was bitterly sarcastic: Do you people enjoy digging graves? he asked.

The tough-minded chief told the other chiefs and warriors at the council that he had selected the most difficult route through Yellowstone. They would not travel the normal hunting trails through the area, but instead would begin at a place called Piton

Kisuit, where two immense rocks mark the beginning of a tortu-
ous mountain trail which was unknown to most men, white or
Indian. They would mount this trail at the same grueling pace
they had followed on the prairie—12 to 14 hours a day climbing
east to Yellowstone Lake and Pelican Valley, then straight north
through Clark's Fork.

The next day, the mad race resumed. The tribe entered Yellowstone, already a national park, and passed hurriedly through the
unearthly beauties of this area. There were giant geysers of
"shooting waters," smaller pots that belched a sulphurous steam,
and warm springs in which, in better times, the Indian men had
alternately soaked and then plunged into the frozen water of nearby streams. In Firehole Canyon, the young were left breathless at
the sight of the circular hole, about one mile in diameter, with
nearly one thousand hot springs and geysers weirdly gurgling or
hissing and shooting steam up to 30 feet in the air.

Along the way, the tribe captured a long-time prospector in the
area, John Shively. When he was questioned, the Indian leaders
realized that Shively knew the new parkland very well, so they
offered him the opportunity to guide the tribe and save his life.
Shively was stunned at the speed the Indians sustained for hours
with minimal rest and nourishment. Hundreds of people and thousands of horses were moved steadily and safely along narrow deer
trails and rocky creek beds. Often, there was barely room on the
trail for two horses abreast, but their progress was determined and
uncomplaining as they headed rapidly eastward toward the Yellowstone River.

Near Mud Holes, a narrow area pocked by bubbling red mud
craters, the Nez Perces captured a party of Helena tourists who
had come to view the splendors of the newly proclaimed Yellowstone Park. Even the hard-headed Poker Joe saw no merit in
killing this group, which included two women. The women were
put under the protection of Joseph, and their young brother was
assigned to the older Nez Perces women to fetch water for them.
The three older men in the white party attempted an escape shortly after their capture, but only two were successful—the other was

*The soldiers fought from the breastworks in the trees
at the Camas Meadows battleground.*

badly wounded and left for dead. He survived to be picked up by Howard's scouts, as were the women and their brother, who were given one horse, some food, and shown the direction they should follow to meet Howard's oncoming troops.

The young man had been well-taken care of by the old women and, in many respects, seemed to have enjoyed his misfortune. Unlike his sisters, he was curious and unintimidated by the experience of "living with savages." He worked willingly, ate the food offered him, and he reported that after a time, he was left alone to roam the large camp. Although he could find no apparent order to the operation of the camp, he was impressed by its smooth functioning. He talked to Shively, who was also very complimentary about the organization, determination and assurance of the tribe despite its tragedy at Big Hole and the relentless pursuit by almost all available troops in the area. Shively escaped the Nez Perces a short time later and repeated for reporters his admiration for the order and discipline of the tribe's retreat through the Yellowstone.

The march north through the Yellowstone became a game of hide-and-seek with white soldiers. At one point, troops were detected on both flanks of the tribe. To the left, going up the Grand Canyon of the Yellowstone, General Howard hurried to outpace the Indians and cut them off at Yellowstone River Valley to the northeast. His strategy was to meet Captain Fisher, marching 82 men along the right flank of the tribe, and to close a noose around the Indians. The shrewd Nez Perce scouts assessed the situation and reported to Poker Joe, who promptly ordered a forced march by the tribe throughout one whole night. By morning, the Nez Perces found themselves well outside General Howard's trap, and after nearly two weeks in the exhausting terrain of the new national park, the Indians finally emerged from the Yellowstone and into Yellowstone River Valley a couple of days ahead of Howard's troops.

The progress of the soldiers at this point was equally heroic. They had been driven by a determined General Howard through a terrain of rock, broken timber and high ridges. The Indian scouts had watched the soldiers labor in shifts all through the day and into the night. They were fascinated by the dedication and ingenuity of these white men who even lowered whole wagons down rocky cliffs with ropes in order to carry out their responsibility to stop the Nez Perces.

The Nez Perces did all they could to divert the relentless General Howard and his troops. The passage through the Yellowstone became an almost ceaseless raiding party. Baronet's bridge was burned, as was Henderson's ranch. A party of white fishermen was attacked and one man was killed. Three men were shot at the end of Clark's Fork; four miners were ambushed and killed somewhere along a creek; Cochran's ranch was raided, with a loss of two lives and all the horses to the Indians. The majority of these victims were acting formally as messengers and scouts for the several Army troops now pursuing the Nez Perces. Poker Joe knew this and considered them honorable prey for his warriors. In fact, because of these raids and killings, the communication system of Howard's army was in constant turmoil and uncertainty.

When the Nez Perces entered the Yellowstone Valley, they felt secure in making an early camp. The elders and chiefs were eager for a full council; for complaints had begun piling up regarding Poker Joe's leadership. He had never relented his pace. He seemed to be everywhere, tall on his horse, shouting orders, demanding greater speed, fewer rests, lighter rations. He hovered over his depressed and exhausted people like a slavemaster.

Most of his tribesmen realized that Poker Joe's methods were largely responsible for their freedom and survival, but they were unaccustomed to and resentful of such rigidity. They were also tired, unbearably tired, and fearful of the future. It was already September, the days were getting shorter and the Indians could smell and feel the coming of winter. This was the hunting and gathering season, time to jerk beef and salmon, to make hardened slabs of kouse, to repair the teepees and clothing, to preserve dried berries and the last crop of blue camas bulbs. Survival through the long winter months depended on the many tasks of September, yet they could not stop to do any of them. They had no reserves—

everything had been lost at Big Hole and Clearwater—and they were worried about the frozen and barren winters on the northern plains.

Poker Joe bluntly asked for a vote on his role as commander; he didn't like argument Indian-style. Since Poker Joe would not speak, Chief Joseph and his brother Ollokut supported his views in the council. The Christian General, they said, would never rest in peace until he had won this war or had lost the Nez Perces over the Canadian border. He would pursue the tribe mercilessly, follow any cruel strategy, to accomplish his goal. Such is the pride and the thirst of white warriors, Joseph said, and of those who would make the Nez Perces into Christians. Joseph and Ollokot reminded their tribesmen that their enemy is both a hardened warrior and a dedicated Christian.

At last, encouraged by Joseph, the chiefs and warriors again nominated Poker Joe as leader of their desperate migration. Still, there was much bad feeling in the camp. The young men were frustrated by the continual running, more like common prey than honorable warriors. Many of the women and children were exhausted and even ill from the weeks of constant passage from sunrise to sunset, with little food and no shelter. Great numbers of horses had been injured or simply abandoned when they became too fatigued to be useful. The Indians had eluded the white general with the strategy of Poker Joe, but the ordeal was increasingly wearing at their will to continue and to fight.

The Nez Perces crossed the Yellowstone River at this point.

*The canyon in Yellowstone Park where General Howard's troops
lowered their wagons by rope and then hauled them up the opposite side.*

9.

A Final Siege at Alikos Pah

AS the Nez Perces hurried toward the Musselshell River in order to reach the Missouri and a familiar trail north to Canada, scouts suddenly warned of soldiers riding hard after them. The troops were led by a Colonel Sturgis, who had been outmaneuvered and outrun by the Nez Perces in the Yellowstone and was under considerable pressure from the general to redeem himself. Sturgis drove his force through a cold rain for nearly 60 miles in one endless day, and the next morning he had the troops up and into their saddles before dawn.

At about the same time that the Nez Perces scouting party reported the approach of the Army, an Army scout had brought word that the Nez Perces were merely a few miles up-river. The tribe was going north and would have to pass through a narrow canyon. A wild horse race followed as both the Indians and the soldiers aimed at getting to the neck of the canyon first. Finally, the Indians reached a vantage point along the canyon wall and the rear guard scouts were able to position themselves for sniping. Colonel Sturgis' troops dismounted and were pinned down by the rifle fire.

The Nez Perces party was astonished to discover that the Crows —their erstwhile allies—were fighting alongside the soldiers. The Nez Perces were also somewhat relieved as it turned out; for the large force of Crows proved to be more interested in the Nez Perces' herds of horses than they were in pursuing General Howard's goals. After a very brief skirmish, the Crows began abandoning their positions in large groups, hoping to flank the Nez Perces sharpshooters. The Crow strategy was unsuccessful—they took only a few dozen horses. But their desertion sufficiently weakened Colonel Sturgis' force so that he felt it necessary to abandon any hope of a further offensive. Three soldiers died; eleven were wounded; and three old Indians were killed, one of them by Crows. It hadn't been the battle that Howard and Sturgis had expected.

Poker Joe took the tribes over Judith Cap, passing between two chains of mountains. There was a shorter route, but snow was already visible on these higher ranges. He knew that the whole area would soon be impassable, immersed in the deep and silent snow and barren of all life. They were in a race against the winter, 200 miles from Canada and safety. Poker Joe estimated that if the snow did not fall and the tribe maintained its present pace, they could cover the rugged countryside in a week.

When they came in sight of the Missouri, Poker Joe led them to a settlement called Cow's Landing, one of the few fording places for miles around. It was a landing for steamers, mainly carrying provisions and ammunition for all the Army forts nearby: Fort Keogh, Custer, Smith, and a few smaller outposts. Ollokot entered the area first with 20 warriors. The small engineering detachment of 13 soldiers quickly hid themselves behind doors and barricades in preparation for a battle, but after a few shots rang here and there, hurting no one, the Indian warriors coolly moved downstream several hundred yards and tested the crossing. A handful of the warriors were behind to watch the soldiers and to guard the main body of the tribe, which had begun to cross the river.

During the fording, some of the Indian scouts returned to the barricaded soldiers to ask them for food. The Nez Perces women had made the best of their four hours of rest each day to gather whatever food they could. They always came up with something: tea leaves, a few camas, kouses, wild mushrooms, some roots known only to the older women. The children pursued small game with bows and arrows, and the warriors hunted when they could, but the tribe was hungry and desperately worried about the imminent snowfall and the barren landscape of winter.

The small engineering detachment couldn't hope to take the offensive against 200 Indian warriors, so the officers threw some bacon and a pack of hard tack to the Nez Perces scouts. However, the scouts had taken note of Army warehouses along the riverfront and the tons of goods which had just recently been unloaded and were stacked in front of the buildings. The scouts returned to the camp and told the council that stores of food and perhaps even weapons were available at Cow's Landing. The chiefs agreed to an immediate raid, and later that evening, the entrenched soldiers watched in horror as the whole troop of Indian warriors recrossed the Missouri and headed straight at them. The soldiers fired a few token shots and then abandoned the settlement.

The looting continued late into the night. The women joined the warriors and stormed through the warehouses, picking at everything, tasting things, packing them into neat piles and loading them on the pack horses. The tribe was as happy as children in a toyshop. They took all the foodstuffs they could carry—flour, sugar, coffee, bacon, hard tack—and the women grabbed kettles and other implements. Poker Joe advised his people not to overload themselves and the horses, but he was unanimously ignored. After the goods were removed from the warehouses, the rearguard scouts set the buildings afire. The tribe watched them burn from across the river, while the morning sun began warming the countryside.

After the event at Cow's Landing, the dark mood of the tribe changed. They wouldn't be pushed any longer. They were no longer hungry. There was happiness and laughter and games. The women prepared a large meal, despite Poker Joe's protest and he watched in anger and astonishment as his tribesmen stuffed their stomachs until they could barely move. He spent the next morning trying to arouse them to continue the march, but they were slow to move. In a rage, Poker Joe rushed to Joseph, pointing out the dangers of delay, but Joseph replied that he could do nothing. Just look at them, said Joseph, pointing at the families eating and talking heartily together. They live like people again. Poker Joe was not appeased: The soldiers won't know the difference, he said.

The camp finally moved again, very late in the morning. There was no concern for the danger of their situation. They were confident that General Howard was far to the rear, and they had no thoughts that other troops might be bearing down upon them. The scouts had left their advance V position to gather and travel with

*The entrance to Canyon Creek Gorge where the Nez Perces
fought off Colonel Sturgis' troops.*

their families. All but Poker Joe, Joseph, and a few council chiefs were confident that there was no need to hurry the remaining 80 miles to Canada. They weren't going to rush any more. They needed rest and time to gather meat and buffalo robes for the winter. The horses needed a chance to fatten up before the snows came. When Poker Joe continued to protest, the council replaced him with Looking Glass.

From Cow's Landing to the Bear Paw Mountains, barely 50 or 60 miles, the tribe dallied along the trail for a full week under Looking Glass's command. The same distance would have taken a day and a half under Poker Joe. Instead of starting each day's march as soon as the sun rose, the Indians slept a little longer or returned to their small canvas shelters for an hour or two of conversation and eating. Looking Glass would ask them to begin, but he did not have Poker Joe's rough, insistent manner and drill-sergeant voice. Sometimes, the Nez Perces would not begin their trek until the middle of the morning, and then they would proceed at a leisurely pace. Looking Glass also failed to ask scouts to fan out ahead of the tribe. Warriors drifted off on their own, hunting for a day or two and leaving the main camp undermanned.

The Nez Perces arrived after a week at a place called "Tsanim Alikos Pah," or "Place of Manure Fire." They stopped there near Snake Creek and set up camp for a few days, perhaps more for nostalgic reasons and for comfort than for the practical ones of security and defense. Alikos Pah was a broad, grassy plain threaded with mountain streams and flanked by timbered buttes. The name of the grassland came from the large quantity of dried buffalo manure found there. In former days, the land had ranged thousands of deer, antelope and buffalo, and it had long served the surrounding tribes as a hunting ground and a gathering place for their winter fuel of buffalo chips.

The Indians had decided to camp at Alikos Pah in order to search out the scarce buffalo and gather some meat and skins. Several in the council thought that the tribe ought to continue and to cross the 30 or so miles to the border. Standing on one of the buttes, one could actually see the land of the Mother Queen, the Red Mounties,

View across Canyon Creek battlefield.

Sitting Bull, and safety. Yet, optimism was the order of the day. Not one of the scouts had been sent out during the night, and the position of the camp in a small hollow near the creek was exposed to open, gently sloping ground on three sides. A well-respected warrior, Wottolen, told the council of his vision of a forthcoming attack; but with safety less than a day's march away and General Howard miles in the rear, the elders dismissed the immediacy of Wottolen's visionary insight.

On September 29, 1877, the tribe was preparing to make their emigration to Canada. They had collected a good store of meat and robes; they were well-fed and well-rested; the horses were fattened and suitable for trade with Sitting Bull. Had only one scout been sent a few miles north that evening, he would have detected an army of 600 soldiers and 200 Crow and Cheyenne Indians waiting in the cold night drizzle with their commander Colonel Miles. They were planning an attack for the following morning.

Miles and his troops were not under the command of General Howard, but had been summoned by the general via telegraphic lines, to cut off the northward escape of the Nez Perces. The troops had been force-marched from Fort Keogh along the Missouri toward Cow's Landing. When the Colonel got word of the attack at Cow's Landing, he ferried his troops across the river and raced after the Nez Perces. He was eager for battle and the likely promotion to general that would be his reward if he succeeded where the Christian General had failed.

The following morning, the Nez Perces camp was alert and ready to move toward Canada at a leisurely pace. The canvas shelters they'd lived under for the last few weeks had been taken down and packed on the horses. Babies were put in their "tekash" and hung on the side of riding horses. The women were preparing the food for the day and supervising the games of the small children. Elders sat at ease, blissfully retelling stories of the vast buffalo herds which had once inhabited these prairies.

The first omen of danger came when a small group of young warriors pointed into the distance toward a cloud of dust rising in the air. They assumed a small herd of buffalo were stampeded and thought little of it until, a few minutes later, the cavalry of Colonel Miles appeared, riding at a full gallop toward the unguarded camp.

For a few seconds, the Indian camp was mesmerized by the deafening rumble of the hundreds of charging horses. Then, the warriors, under Ollokot and Too-Hool, quickly came to their senses and set up a line of defense just below the crest of a hillock south of the campsite. Some 120 warriors awaited the charge of 600; the remaining 50 or 60 warriors followed Joseph to the herds of horses and began moving them and the noncombatants along the trail toward the Canadian border.

Joseph and his men had moved just in time. A group of Crows had already begun swerving away from Miles' charge and toward the valuable Nez Perces herds. Each of the Crow warriors had been promised five Nez Perces horses by the Army recruiters. The attacking Crows were met and driven back by Joseph's small forces, but not before the major escape route was cut off. Several families had gotten away and were racing toward Canada, but most of the tribe were forced to remain in the valley protected by their warriors.

When the soldiers came within a 100 yards of the Indians, 20 Nez Perces sharpshooters began firing at a desperate pace. Soldier after soldier fell, sometimes in clusters of two or three, and the wounded were screaming above the thunder of the fire. The death rate of the officers was particularly high, and the long line of charging horsemen was soon stopped about 75 yards from the ridge. The soldiers dismounted and barricaded themselves against the murderous fire. Both lines held for the day, and Colonel Miles made no further vainglorious cavalry charges. The new strategy of Miles was quite common for an Indian battle at the time: The soldiers were to entrench and keep the warriors busy while the Indian detachments of the Army were left free to harass the fleeing families and steal the horses of the Indian camp.

Miles made a few attempts to outflank the Nez Perces and to cut them off from the water supply, but each time, small groups of sharpshooters held the soldiers down. Even so, a few small groups of Nez Perces braves had been cut off from the main force; and, tragically, several warriors, including Poker Joe, were killed by rifle fire from Nez Perces Chief Husi-Husi-Cute and his fighters.

As darkness fell, both sides began to dig in. On the Nez Perces side, the entire night was spent digging trenches in the damp earth, very deep ones for the women, children and elderly, waist-high shelters for the warriors. The women and the elders did most of the digging with knives, yet they succeeded in constructing an amazing web of interconnected trenches and tunnels. During the night, the chiefs also dispatched a small group of warriors to ride north and ask the assistance of Sitting Bull.

That night was as nightmarish for the Nez Perces as the seige at Big Hole. The trenches and pits were quite damp, and few of the Indians had had time to collect extra clothing or food during the attack. Children were huddled against the women in the deep pit to keep them warm and stop their crying. Small fires were made with buffalo chips which the women had gathered by crawling through the grass on their hands and knees. The courageous young warriors collected water for their people by repeatedly venturing into the darkness while hanging on the flanks of their horses and dragging buffalo horns through the creek.

An assessment of the battle losses revealed that between 20 and 25 of the warriors had been killed, and many more wounded. Ollokot had been fatally shot while holding back one side of the soldiers' position by himself from behind a small rock. His body remained on the battlefield; the grief-stricken Joseph had been unable to reach the site before sundown.

The deaths of Poker Joe and Ollokot proved a heavy blow to the tribe's confidence. In the course of the night, the nearest soldiers could hear the strange chants for the dead blending with the crying of cold and hungry children and wounded braves. Some of the surviving warriors were crazed by the stress and were talking to themselves, daydreaming about the beautiful Wallowa Valley— the land of the blue camas, the pronghorns, the mountain streams and Guardian Spirits. Others tried to climb out of the trenches, shouting hysterically for vengeance against the soldiers.

Colonel Miles attacked the Nez Perces at this point on Snake Creek.

*Point of Rocks, where Indian sharpshooters
repulsed Colonel Miles's cavalry charge.*

Many of the Indian families were doubly stung, suffering not only with fear and cold and the loss of fallen friends and relatives, but also with the anguish of separation from the loved ones who had already been on the trail at the time of the attack and were cut off by the battle. Joseph's wife and daughter were among those cut off, and now, as far as the great chief knew, they were either under pursuit by soldiers, or dead, or making their way through the snow toward Canada.

When morning came, a cold, heavy snow was falling. There was little shooting that morning, and by mid-day, the battlefield was an unmarred, eerily silent expanse of white. This perfection was not to last for long. Since the storm prevented any pitched fighting, Miles ordered his artillery unit to shell the Indian camp and trenches.

Colonel Miles was at odds with himself to make the right decision. He knew that he could not pursue a course of charging and fighting these Indians without great losses to his command. At the same time, he was fearful that Sitting Bull might sweep down to the rescue—or, just as regretable, that General Howard might catch up and take all credit for the capture of the Nez Perces. Finally, Miles determined to try to negotiate with the Indians and persuade them to surrender.

Early in the morning, he sent two Christian Nez Perces as messengers to their warrior brothers. As the emissaries approached the Nez Perces line, they shouted: "Surrender, my brothers, and you will be treated well. You have fought well, but now is the time for peace and rest." The warriors respected the white flag, and the intermediaries arranged for a meeting between Miles and Chief Joseph, whom the Colonel had specifically requested. Because Joseph was well-known among the whites as a wise and literate man, they inevitably assumed, like Miles, that the chief was the military leader of the Nez Perces. The two men met between the fighting camps. Tom Hill translated.

Colonel Miles asked that the Indians stack their guns and surrender.

In return for what? asked Joseph.

Good treatment!

Chief Ollokut was killed while firing from behind this rock.

*Burial pit where both Indians and soldiers
killed in the battle were buried.*

Shall we return home?

Maybe, but I can make no promises.

We want a promise first, Joseph said, and then we'll surrender only half of our guns. We need the others to hunt the buffalo. We have no food.

Of course, Miles could make no such promise. Moreover, he had been schooled as an Army officer to treat with warring Indians only in unconditional terms. The two men separated briefly, but then, still under the white flag of truce, Colonel Miles had Joseph arrested and rushed into the Army camp. There, Joseph was hobbled, rolled in two blankets, and placed in a sheltered area near the pack mules. Joseph was left all night in this manner, but Miles' hope of demoralizing the Indians and forcing their surrender was stymied by a twist of fate the following morning. One of the Army officers, Lieutenant Jerome, had wandered out of sheer curiosity near the Nez Perces camp and was made a prisoner. The angry Colonel Miles had to return Joseph in exchange for his lieutenant, who would have been killed that day if Joseph hadn't returned.

As soon as Joseph returned to the Nez Perces camp, the exchange of gunfire resumed with even greater intensity, and Miles ordered up a fierce bombardment of the Indian lines. However, neither side left its position or attempted an offensive drive. Miles was cautious; he had already lost one-fourth of his force in deaths or casualties. For their part, the Indians were exhausted and discouraged. They waited in the hope that Sitting Bull's Sioux warriors would come to their aid.

Life in the Indian camp was becoming grim. Food was scarce; blankets and robes were also rare, as many of the fallen warriors had been honored with a shroud for burial. The chiefs held council after council, but they could come to no conclusion. Continue north? How could they, with Colonel Miles at their rear and the burden of the herds, the hungry children, the elderly and the wounded. Only the strongest could make it; they would have to abandon the others to the cruelties of the other hostile Indian tribes. Surrender? How could they trust any white man's word again after all their treaties had been violated?

*Lieutenant Jerome, who was captured by the Indians,
was exchanged for Joseph who was being held hostage by the troops.*

10.

"I Will Fight No More Forever"

THE arrival of General Howard and an advance guard of his large army banished any remaining dreams of victory and rescue. White Bird came to a separate decision. He would flee to Canada with all those who could and would follow him. Looking Glass preferred to hold on to the distant hope that Sitting Bull might yet come. Joseph proposed surrender; the Sioux were a day's ride away and it had been four days since the Nez Perces had sent a messenger to ask for help. Thus, the camp was told that the council was divided into three groups.

From the pits and lines, warriors, women, and children began separating. Many families were broken up when brothers chose differently and sons left their parents. Most of the horses were given to White Bird, who had 140 men and boys and 93 women and young girls. As a rule, only the fittest followed White Bird; they all knew the hardships to be endured on such a journey. They also knew that the soldiers would pursue them. Some were on horseback, many more were on foot, as they pushed northward in silence, under the cover of night and a snowfall.

After the departure of White Bird, Looking Glass and Joseph were still at odds as to the fate of the remaining tribesmen. If you surrender, Looking Glass exclaimed in council, you will be sorry; and in your sorrow, you will wish rather to be dead, than suffer the deception white men will surely deliver. But then in a moment of supreme irony, Looking Glass suddenly climbed out of his fighting pit and pointed toward an Indian riding in the distance. There, he shouted, help is coming. The next moment, Looking Glass was dead, shot by that lone Indian, who was not one of Sitting Bull's warriors but rather a Cheyenne scout fighting for Miles and Howard.

Joseph no longer hesitated. He saw his forlorn people; he saw the impossible odds of their heroic struggle. Nothing in the world, not even the ground of his beloved Wallowa Valley, could change his mind. He had not had much voice in the conduct of the war, because he was, like his father, a peace chief. Following the ancient customs of his tribe, he had obeyed the rules. But now, he was solely responsible for his people—for those who remained—and mere survival seemed the only possible and the only important option. They would lose a war; they would lose their land and their dignity; but they would survive.

Before riding out with a white flag, Joseph told his people they still had the choice and time to get out if they wished. Then he sent a messenger to General Howard, asking the terms of surrender. Howard promised to return the tribe to Lapwai in the spring, when the wounded were whole and the deep snows had melted. With that promise, Joseph rode that morning, with two warriors at his side, to a butte. There, with a quiver in his voice, Tom Hill translated the poignant surrender speech which Chief Joseph had given at the final war council:

> Tell General Howard I know his heart. What he told me before, I have it in my heart. I am tired of fighting. Our chiefs are killed. Looking Glass is dead. Too-Hool-Hool-Zute is dead. The old men are dead. It is the young men now who say "yes" or "no." He who led the young men, my brother, is dead. It is cold and we have no blankets. The little children are freezing to death. My people, some of them, have run away to the hills and have no blankets, no food. No one knows where they are —perhaps freezing to death. I want to have time to look for my children and see how many of them I can find. Maybe I shall find them among the dead. Hear me, my chiefs. I am tired; my heart is sick and sad. From where the sun now stands, I will fight no more forever.

The three Indians then rode to the line of waiting officers and Joseph quickly dismounted. He walked to the two men and held out his rifle as a gesture of surrender. General Howard made a sign that Colonel Miles should receive the surrender. Joseph handed Miles the rifle, then pulled his blanket across his face, in a sign of shame and defeat. Behind him, 87 men, 184 women and 147 children followed in silence. The proud Nez Perces were vanquished. All that could be heard across that broad, empty plain were the voices of white soldiers. It was as if that rich and ancient Indian heritage had suddenly passed, like an echo in the wind.

Colonel Miles, soon to be made a general, wired his superiors in Washington: "We have had our usual success. We made a direct and rapid march across the country. After a severe engagement, being under fire for three days, the hostile camp, under Chief Joseph, surrendered at two o'clock today." This unnecessary and tragic war was over—after four months, a cost to the United States government of nearly a million dollars, and the deaths of 127 soldiers, 50 white civilians, and approximately 151 Nez Perces.

The Indians were transported almost immediately to nearby Fort Keogh; but before they had departed, they witnessed a final humiliation. All of the Indian scouts who had been allied with the Army against the Nez Perces were allowed to select five horses from among the Nez Perces herds. Then, stripped of their possessions and their dignity, the Nez Perces were taken away.

They expected to remain at Keogh for the winter and then to be returned to the Lapwai Reservation in the spring. Such had been the promise of both Miles and Howard. But despite the protests of the two officers, who had come to respect and admire this courageous tribe, the government preferred to send the Nez Perces, first, to Fort Lincoln, 800 miles away in the Dakota Territory, because it would be cheaper to accommodate the Indians there; and then, after a few weeks, to the Indian Territory (now Oklahoma), where they would be far from other rebellious bands in the Northwest and where they would be forced by circumstances and survival to settle down to farming.

Fort Leavenworth, in Indian Territory, was at first a devastating experience for the Nez Perces. More than one-quarter of the tribe were wiped out within a few months by malaria and other diseases resulting from the poor location and sanitary conditions of the camp. Once they became acclimated to the site, however, the Nez Perces regained their strength and—in their typically industrious way—made a remarkable success of their farmlands and the manufacture and sale of bows and arrows, moccasins, gloves and

A disheartened Joseph surrenders to Colonel Miles.

finely worked leather clothing. They also began herding again and had soon built up a large stock of horses and cattle.

Each year they petitioned the government to return them to cool mountain air and rushing waters of their homeland, but there was little thought in Washington for the exiled tribe until an interview, "Chief Joseph's Own Story," appeared in a national periodical called *North American Review* in 1879. This moving account, in Joseph's own eloquent aboriginal English, was shortly followed by an article and a book by the Christian General. The combination so engaged and aroused the public that the government was finally pressured in 1885 to return this noble people to their beloved homeland in the Wallowa.